Herman & Daphine
Spring 1978

W9-CAR-336

Herman & Daphine
Spring 1978

THE MUSEUMS
OF ISRAEL

1. **The Rockefeller Museum**, Jerusalem

THE MUSEUMS OF ISRAEL

L.Y. RAHMANI
Chief Curator, Israel Department of
Antiquities and Museums
Photographs by PETER LARSEN

Secker & Warburg, London

Acknowledgements

We gratefully acknowledge the permission granted by the Israel Department of Antiquities and Museums to reproduce the objects here illustrated, with the exception of the following whose owners must also be thanked: Israel Museum, Jerusalem, pl. 42; Ha'aretz Museum, Tel-Aviv, pls. 188-91; Museum of Ancient Art, Haifa, pls. 202-204, 209; Dagon, Haifa, pls. 216, 219; Sha'ar Ha-golan, pl. 260; Basilica of the Annunciation, Nazareth, pl. 259; Sdot Yam, pl. 271; Islamic Museum, Jerusalem, pls. 115, 117-8, 121.

All photographs are by Peter Larsen, except for the following, and we should like to thank those who supplied them: Israel Department of Antiquities and Museums, pls. 2, 19, 30, 62, 239, 256; Israel National Parks Authority, pl. 268; Israel Museum, Jerusalem, pls. 10-11, 36, 47, 56, 65, 72-4, 83, 86-9, 91-2, 94, 96-7, 293; Beersheba Municipal Museum, pl. 234; L. A. Mayer Institute of Islamic Art, Jerusalem, pls. 281-2; Mishkan le-Omanut, En Harod, pls. 246, 249, 252; Dagon, Haifa, pls. 219-20; Rybak House, Bat Yam, pl. 233; Professor Y. Yadin, pl. 48.

First published in England 1976 by
Martin Secker & Warburg Limited
14 Carlisle Street, London W1V 6NN

Frontispiece: The Rockefeller Museum, Jerusalem

SBN: 436 24238 9

Designed by Graham Keen

Printed in Great Britain by W & J Mackay Limited, Chatham
by photo-litho

Contents

Foreword   7

Historical Background   11

Museums of Jerusalem   15
   The Rockefeller and Israel Museums   15
   Other Jerusalem Museums   104

Museums of Tel Aviv   115
   The Tel Aviv and Ha'aretz Museums   115

The Museums of Haifa   160
   Municipal and Other Museums   160

Museums of Other Cities   173
   Nahariyyah, Acre, Tiberias, Beth Shean, Bat Yam, Beersheba   173

District Museums   184
   Beth Ussishkin, Hanitha, Beth Sturman, Mishkan le-Omanut,
   Ohel Sarah, Midreshet Ruppin   184

Local and Site Museums   197
   Palamahim, Nazareth, Sha'ar Ha-Golan, Hazor, Beth Shearim,
   Megiddo, Masada, Sdot Yam, Caesarea   197

Specialized Museums   221
   Wilfrid Israel House of Oriental Art, Mediterranean Archaeology;
   Mayer Institute of Islamic Art   221

History Museums   227
   Herzl, Petah Tiqva and Aaronson House Museums; the Memorials of
   Lohamei Hageta'ot, Yad Vashem and Yad Mordekhai   227

Chronological Table   239

2

FOREWORD

In any given country museums tend to express the cultural and ideological interests of the people. This seems to be true even in countries whose major museums stem from the collections of their former rulers, who wanted to amass costly and rare objects for their own delight, to impress and overawe visitors, and to ensure the value of their treasures. We find that interest shifts to emphasize the national and cultural aspects of a country. In some countries, the main interest will be painting in general and local schools in particular; in others local folklore and culture; others again seem specially taken by problems of technology, science and natural history. It is self-evident that correlations exist between national, social and political problems and cultural interest. Museum directors who disregard this rule often find that their museums are not popular with the local people, even if the tourist-trade masks this fact by filling their museums with bus-loads of foreigners. This rule is especially true in small countries such as Israel, where little or nothing was collected by bygone potentates. Here, museums, the majority of which were established since 1948, point clearly to the Jewish people's interest in two major aspects of their intellectual and emotional preoccupations: all that is connected with the history of its ancient homeland and its own history, and cultural achievement throughout its prolonged and world-wide Diaspora.

Described here are some of the initial steps undertaken by Israel to create a network of sixty museums, all but eight begun in the twenty-five years of Israel's renewed statehood. Zionist pioneers and Catholic monks, British governors and Moslem sheikhs, kibbutz members and private collectors, learned institutions, foreign and local benefactors, municipal, regional and governmental bodies have all taken part in their establishment; they have now become a tan-

2. **Eric Gill** (1882–1940) *Relief* (1937) Jerusalem. Height 1.90 m. limestone (**R**) This relief, made by Eric Gill for the Rockefeller Museum, today graces the tympanum above this museum's main entrance. It perfectly expresses the fundamental fact of this country's history: its position between Africa and Asia.

gible expression of a young state, a very ancient people and a diversified population.

The reader is introduced to the museums by means of a short text and as many pictures as could reasonably be put into one volume. The aim is to summarize some of their contents, to give pictorial examples, and point out their archaeological, historical and artistic significance. In choosing the archaeological examples we have tried to give preference to finds shown in the local museums rather than similar artifacts displayed in larger museums. Sites have been included only if they have a museum open to the public.

It is our pleasurable duty to thank the Director of the Department of Antiquities and Museums, Mr A. Eitan, for his permission to include state-owned antiquities—in fact all those illustrated here, unless otherwise stated. Our special thanks go to Dr H. Gamzu, Director of the Tel Aviv Museum, and his Assistant-Curator, Mrs Nehama Goralnik; to Mrs Elisheva Cohen, Chief-Curator, and Mr Y. Fisher, Curator at the Israel Museum, Jerusalem, and to Mr Z. Efron, Director of Mishkan le-Omanut at En Harod, for having put their great knowledge of art in general, and Jewish and Israeli art in particular, at our disposal. It goes without saying that any error and omission, as well as opinions expressed, are our own.

Sincere thanks are due to Mrs Irene Lewitt and Miss E. Rubin of the Photographic Department of the Israel Museum and to its curators, as well as to the directors and curators of the museums mentioned in this book for their help in making our work possible. The author's thanks are due, too, to the photographer, Mr Peter Larsen for his large part in the origination of this book, and for his valuable suggestions in the wording of the text. Final and personal thanks are extended to the author's friend and colleague, Mrs M. Divoire of Brussels, who most generously spent part of her annual vacation in editing the manuscript.

The dynamic development of Israel will have inevitably added new museums, new pavilions and new exhibitions to existing ones even as this book goes to press. Both readers and the museums' curators must forgive us if mention of these is lacking. We hope this book will encourage the reader to visit Israel's museums, where he will then have the added pleasure of discovery. If it helps him to that enjoyment, we will be much gratified.

3. Cult Stand (tenth century BC)
Ashdod. Height 0.35 m. pottery **(IM)**
The upper part of this stand still has
traces of a painted decoration in the
Philistine tradition. Its lower part has
figurines of five musicians: players of the
double-flute, the lyre, cymbals, and
(not shown in the photo) another
double-flute and a tambourine. A local
cult scene seems to have been represented, similar to those enacted in front
of early prophets (*cf.* 1. Sam. 10:15) or
by Levites in the ritual of the Solomonic
Temple (2 Chron. 5:12–13).

HISTORICAL BACKGROUND

4. The Annunciation Flask (sixth century AD) unknown provenance. Height 0.10 m. pottery **(IM)** Such flasks (*ampullae*) were brought home by Christian pilgrims, filled either with oil from lamps that were burned in front of shrines, with water from some nearby source, or with earth from a holy place. The image and the inscription together were regarded as having beneficial, indeed prophylactic, properties. The ampulla here shown has on both its faces the identical representation of Mary seated on a high-backed chair, spinning, the winged Angel appearing from the right, hand raised in salutation, pronouncing the opening words of the Annunciation (Luke 1:28) which appear in Greek around the relief: 'Hail, thou art highly favoured, the Lord is with thee!' The scene and inscription suggest Nazareth, where the foundations of a fifth- to sixth-century church have been discovered, as the place of manufacture and origin (see pl. 258).

Between Africa and Asia, bordered by the sea and the desert, lies Israel, the land-bridge connecting two huge continents. It has carried through the ages man's fights and trades, his arts and faiths, and the many tokens of love, of hate and of hope, some ephemeral and others eternal.

Many people passed over it, most of them to hasten on to conquests beyond: ancient Egyptians, for whom it was a foothold against the 'miserable Asiatics'; ancient western Asiatics: Amorites, Horites, Hyksos, Mitanni, Hittites and Habiru; and eventually the Assyrians, Babylonians and Persians, who used it as a base against Egypt, some for shorter raids and some for prolonged conquest. For many of these, it was known as the Land of Canaan, named after the inhabitants of its northern shores. Some of these conquerors and many another tribe of different ethnic origin, some of Semitic language and some of Aryan, would eventually settle the country's fertile plains and wooded mountains and dwell there for a while: build, strive, worship their tribal gods or take over some local deity—and eventually vanish, absorbed by new-comers, the ruins of their dwellings and the remains of their artifacts adding another layer to the country's ancient sites.

In the flow of its history, this strip of land became a bridge-head for trader and conqueror from the West, here too the flag often following the trade: 'sea-people' from Asia Minor and the Aegean, including the coast-dwelling Philistines, who would bequeath the name Palestine to the country, even after having themselves vanished from its history. After them came Greek mercenaries, Macedonian and Roman conquerors, to be eventually followed by many Europeans: those following the Cross in the eleventh century, those following the Tricolor at the end of the eighteenth, and those carrying the Union Jack in the twentieth. Throughout all these periods, these fertile lands were swamped by periodic waves of nomads from the eastern deserts. Some came only to loot, returning to their native land; others to settle, partly replacing the existing population and partly mingling with it, their offspring eventually to become the prey of some future raid from the same quarter. Periodically, too, came mighty waves of conquest from the East and North-East: Persian and Arab, Mongol and Turk, some to settle, most to pass on to further conquests in Africa, Asia Minor and Europe.

Among all the tribes, traders and warriors to tread upon this land, only one clung to it, seeing in it the fulfilment of an ancient and divine promise of an eternal home; they called it by the name which, according to tradition, the Lord bestowed upon its tribal forefather Jacob—Israel, 'the One who strove with God'.

In the first quarter of the thirteenth century BC these Israelites began to settle in the country, becoming a patriarchal and tribal society, forming some three centuries later a united kingdom, but one that was to split into two smaller ones after only two generations. Twice they would build a temple to their God whom only they, of all the nations and religions, defined as the one and only true God, without image or conceivable form.

For their capital they chose the place which, according to their lore, the Lord chose as his dwelling place: a somewhat arid spot, off the highways that crossed the land-bridge—the ancient city of Salem. It was built between a rocky 'high place' (that is, a place of worship on high ground), dedicated since time immemorial to the worship of a godhead, and a life-giving source of water, hallowed spot for a king's anointment. Eventually they changed its name to Yerushalayim—Jerusalem, 'City of Peace'.

City and temple were destroyed twice: in 586 BC and AD 70; but though driven from their soil, the Jews would continue to dwell in their land—if only in their songs and prayers, and in their dreams of return. As, invariably, they did, overcoming every obstacle. Their forefathers were buried on the slopes of the mountains facing the sacred temple mount, in tombs dating from the early seventh century BC and continuing to our days; people of one culture, one religion and one ethnic background, whose headstones carried inscriptions in one language which is still read and used—Hebrew. In this city and land, the belief in one God would evolve into Judaism, its precepts taught by prophets and sages; it would foster Christianity, brought by some of its sons to the world of the Gentiles; and it would serve as an inspiration to Islam, teaching the belief in one supreme and compassionate Deity.

The soil of the land preserved the relics of all those who had passed over it—for a trader's market-day, a battle encounter, a century's or a millennium's conquest and settlement. In later days, some of these were unearthed and taken away, to be kept in foreign lands and their museums.

Meanwhile the Jewish people had started their long wandering in a world-wide Diaspora, seldom permitted to stay for any length of time

in one spot, saving in times of persecution and ever-recurring exile two valuables only, which for them spelled life itself: their children and their Torah, the book of laws and lore.

Until fairly recently, the ancient land of Israel remained without a museum to keep even its own relics, while the people of Israel had nowhere, up to the latter part of the last century, to display those articles of their own cultural heritage which had not been looted from them in recurring persecutions. During the last world war destruction and looting demolished many Jewish museums in Central and Eastern Europe. After the War, only part of their collections could be saved, to be exhibited in local museums of folklore and religion, often as reminders of a people that had virtually ceased to exist. Only a few Jewish museums in Europe escaped this fate. The Jews of the New World, mainly in the United States, were more fortunate, being able to establish their own museums of Jewish culture, folklore, religion and history. These, however, lacked significant material from the land of Israel.

In 1906, Jewish artists returning to their homeland established both an Art School and a National Museum in Jerusalem under the directorship of their teacher, Professor Boris Schatz. They were both named Bezalel, after Bezalel ben Uri of the tribe of Judah, chief artisan of the Tabernacle (Ex. 31). The museum has continued to develop its collection of local natural history and antiquities, and Jewish objects from the Diaspora. After the death of its first director, it was headed by Mordechai Narkiss, from 1932 to his death in 1957. Its contents were transferred to the Israel Museum in 1965. At the same time, some of the Catholic Orders established their own collections, mainly in their centres in Jerusalem. The Franciscans, functioning since the thirteenth century as Custodians of the Holy Land (while all other western Christian establishments in this country date from the mid-nineteenth century or later), established a small collection of local antiquities in 1902. They were followed in Jerusalem by other Orders; however, theirs is the only collection to have developed, since 1931, into a small but fully-fledged museum, still open to the public.

Thus practically all important finds made in this country prior to 1917 found their way into the major museums of Europe, while a few only were retained by the Turkish overlords, most to be deposited at their museum in Istambul, others to become lost in the private collections of the sultan. Only a few items, some too cumbersome to be moved, were left in the country and kept in the Moslem college of el Mamouniyeh, in the old city of Jerusalem, eventually to form the nucleus of a national museum, established by the British Mandatory Power in 1922, in the barracks annexed to that city's Citadel. The enlargement of this nucleus—later to become Jerusalem's Rockefeller Museum—is dealt with in the following chapter.

THE MUSEUMS OF JERUSALEM
THE ROCKEFELLER MUSEUM

The Mandatory Government, with a large endowment made by John D. Rockefeller Jr, transferred its Department of Antiquities and its Archaeological Museum to a magnificent new building which was opened to the public in 1938. It was planned by Austen St Barbe Harrison to be both completely functional and beautifully adapted to its position on a hill overlooking the ancient moat opposite the old city's north-east corner; a hill which enabled Godfrey de Bouillon and his army to invade the city by use of a siege-tower in 1099, overcoming the resistance of both Moslems and Jews.

Behind the museum's modern building stands a spacious house, built by Muhammed el Khalili in 1711, a Hebronite who, it is said, brought a pine seedling from his native city and planted it near his new house. It has now grown into a huge tree which will eventually be included, together with the house, in any future extensions to the museum.

The museum exhibits finds from all the major excavations undertaken in the country between 1920 and 1948, plus a few later additions, while its galleries, stores and extensive library carry comprehensive records of finds and sites—written, drawn and photographed. In 1948 the Jewish members of the staff had to leave the premises. Under the auspices of the Department of Antiquities and Museums, they founded a small museum, housed since 1951 in the same street as the Rockefeller—the two so very near, yet separated by the barbed wire and mine-fields which then divided the city. However, the contents of the latter museum were transferred to the Israel Museum in 1967, while the Department of Antiquities and Museums returned to the Rockefeller building in 1967.

ITEMS IN THE ROCKE-FELLER MUSEUM ARE MARKED (R), THOSE IN THE ISRAEL MUSEUM (IM)

5. Anthropomorphic Rhyton (1750–1550 BC) Jericho. Height 0.21 m. pottery **(R)**
This vessel, found in a tomb at Jericho, shows the head of a Canaanite gentleman of the period, characterized by a sharp nose and pointed beard, reminiscent of contemporary and later Egyptian representations of 'The mighty men of Asia' as described in the story of Sinuhe's sojourn in Israel. This vessel too is executed in the technique characteristic of Tell al-Yahudiyya ware (*cf.* pl. 13).

THE ISRAEL MUSEUM

Since its opening in 1965 this has become Israel's central national museum. Planned by Professor A. Mansfield and Mrs Dora Gad, its pavilions and sculpture garden are sited on a hill which has the Georgian-Crusader, Greek Orthodox Monastery of the Cross to the east, the new campus of the Hebrew University to the west and the Knesset (Parliament) to the north. It contains five major divisions: the **Bezalel National Art Museum**, the **Billy Rose Art Garden**, the **Samuel Bronfman Biblical and Archaeological Museum** (which also administers the archaeological division of the Rockefeller Museum), the **Shrine of the Book** and the **Youth Wing**.

To be comprehensive and avoid repetition a description of the archaeological section of this museum must nowadays include the contents of both the Bronfman and the Rockefeller museums, so that one may quickly grasp as a whole this cross-section of the country's important archaeological finds. (In the picture captions they are marked thus: IM for the Israel Museum and R for the Rockefeller Museum.) Starting with Early Man, some half-million years ago, we encounter Neanderthal-type skulls in Galilee; very much later and after a prolonged process of evolution, some 35–40,000 years ago, we find a man showing Neanderthal and modern features, in

6. Israel Museum, Jerusalem
It contains major finds of local archaeology discovered since 1948, as well as other important collections of antiquities from neighbouring cultures; numismatic collections and antique glass; a central exhibition of Jewish ceremonial art and costumes and European, American and Oriental arts and crafts. Here too are the Dead Sea Scrolls and the Bar Kokhba letters and other valuable manuscripts, some illuminated, a large sculpture garden, an extensive youth wing and a large library.

both Galilee and Carmel caves. This man however also becomes extinct, to be replaced by modern man.

In the seventh millennium BC a new culture emerges, perhaps the first that really deserves to be so designated, bringing with it agriculture and domestication of animals, settlements in villages (in rare cases sufficiently fortified to earn the name of city), figurines, mainly female, pointing to a fertility cult, and skull-burials, perhaps a kind of ancestor-worship. In the Chalcolithic Period (4000–3150 BC) new ethnic groups seem to have entered the country, coming perhaps from beyond the north-eastern borders of Syria. They brought with them a wide range of skills in building techniques, tool-making and in the working of clay, bone, stone and metal, much of it used in the manufacture of cult objects, and all demonstrating an astonishing versatility in techniques and an ability to shape an identical material either into daringly large and heavy forms or small and delicate ones; all this with an unfailing sense of shape and colour. Many finds are witnesses to this skill, among them ossuaries, huge storage jars, and egg-shell-fine bowls so light they can be suspended by a string from a peg—all done in clay (rough or smooth), in coil-construction or turned on a mat. Rough basalt is smoothed down into large and small bowls, offering-stands on an open-work base—all made out of a single block of stone, finally incised with a delicate pattern. Brittle obsidian is worked into jewellery, sometimes with such a smooth surface that it was probably used as a mirror. Bone and ivory are fashioned into a large variety of figurines, in a style sometimes reminiscent of contemporary art of the Nile valley. Copper is hardened with arsenic and cast in the 'lost wax' technique. Remnants of woven material and straw mats prove that these crafts too had been mastered by the people of that period.

The Early Canaanite Period (c. 3150–2200 BC) witnesses the building of fortified towns in the country, including communally organized food supplies (grain storage in silos) and worship (central temples). The same age sees also the first inroads of Egyptians into this 'land of the Retenu' , seeking wood for their ships and buildings, sometimes leaving their tools and weapons in some unexplained hoard or losing them on the trail; similarly, one might also pick up some evidence of traders from the north, as far afield as Anatolia and Mesopotamia.

The end of this period and the beginning of the next, the Middle Canaanite Period (2200–1550 BC), begins with invasions of Amorites, those western Semites who destroyed many of the existing cities of the country and remained for a long period nomadic or semi-nomadic; one finds their family tombs, but not their dwellings. The contents of these tombs can be exhibited. Not so the relics of just one such Semitic family-group of Hebrews—Abraham and his offspring, coming from Ur in southern Mesopotamia to dwell in the southern part of the country. While their family-tomb is purchased for perpetuity near Hebron, they, like their own God, have remained aloof from any tangible and material proof, though living forever in the words of the first book of the Bible.

The city-states re-emerging in the second part of this period are dominated by the Hyksos, the hated 'Asiatics' who invaded and conquered Egypt and became the enemy par excellence of the Egyptians. Their mighty fortifications and excellent pottery vessels, as well as their finely-worked weapons and jewellery, speak of a high level of civilization. The same period sees also the building of temples near the indigenous 'high places', where offerings were brought to some local deity. The latter are however, sometimes represented by small figurines, for domestic rather than temple use.

This period sees the beginning of the Semitic (so-called Proto-Canaanite) alphabetic writing which, with only slight changes, serves us to this day in Hebrew. Many of the letters, turned about-face, have gone into the making of the Greek and subsequently the Latin alphabet.

The Late Canaanite Period (1550–1200 BC) sees a further development of most of these cultural traits, though there was a sharp change in the political picture. The Egyptians, having succeeded in throwing off the Hyksos rule, invaded Canaan and Syria, directly ruling over the local city-states, though clashing in the north with the Hittite Kingdom which was spreading from Anatolia, and whose cultural influence was clearly felt in the north of the country in the temples and 'high places'. This is, moreover, a time of steadily growing pressure from the east and north-east by the Habiru (lit. 'those who pass'), those groups of differing ethnic origins who had left their former dwelling-places and, banded together, had succeeded—often with the help of local city-kings—in entering the country, destroying cities and eventually settling on the land. A fragment of a tablet in cuneiform characters containing a part of the Gilgamesh epic indicates the cultural ties with Mesopotamia, while Cypriot and Mycenaean imports announce the growing influence of Western traders—soon to be followed by the sword.

The Israelite Period (1200–586 BC) was to witness in its first phase the Exodus of Israel from Egypt and its Sojourn in the desert, and though opinions differ about the exact date it is usually placed between 1290 and 1260 BC. Again, we have a complete lack of remains; indeed, all the Israel Museum can show of that period is a huge photo

7. **'Ammud Man** (*c.* 35,000 BC) 'Ammud cave, north-west of Lake Kinneret **(IM)**
These remains of a male aged about twenty-five years belong to the transitional stage between the Middle and Upper Palaeolithic. They show some features of Neanderthal man, later to become extinct; other features already point to Homo Sapiens, man as he exists today. The photo behind the skull, with its heavy eyebrows and protruding jaws, shows the skeleton as it was discovered, while the stone tools he used are shown above.

8

of Mount Sinai facing a photo of Pharaoh Merneptath's stele of 1220 BC, which carries the boast, 'Israel is laid waste, his seed is not'—in essence confronting the declaration of the acceptance of the Eternal Law of the unseen Deity by a people who, their foes declared, had ceased to exist from their very birth as a nation. Strangely enough, both these diametrically opposed declarations have, time and again, been repeated in Israel's history.

At the same time the 'sea-people', Philistines and others, having given battle to the Egyptians under Ramses III—for a while his vassals and garrisons in the country—had established their independent rule, mainly along the southern coast. Their many artifacts—sarcophagi, pottery, weapons, cult-objects—found in cities and tombs, speak of a civilization that was to be overcome by Israel, first in pitched battles, later by a slow process of absorption. At this period the Canaanites were touched by Western influences and these too became absorbed into their own traditions.

From the tenth century BC onwards we find another people of growing influence on the north coast—the Phoenicians, descendants of the Northern Canaanite trading cities: Aradus, Byblos, Tyre, Sidon and Acre, originally known respectively as Arwad, Geval, Tzor, Tzidon and Acco. Merchants and artisans, the Phoenicians traded goods with their neighbours farther inland and from distant coastal regions, gathering styles from Egypt, Mesopotamia, Syria, Anatolia and the

8. Pithos and Jar (4000–3200 BC) **(IM)**

The large pithos, 1.50 metres high, comes from the Jordan valley. It was built up from coils of coarse and gritty clay; the impression of the mat upon which it was fashioned can still be seen on its base. The rope decoration is thought to be a copy of the actual ropes which were wound around large vessels such as this to add to their stability. The delicate 'cream-ware' jar nearby comes from Beersheba. Its height is 0.13 metres and it is hand-made from a very fine whitish clay containing Negev kaolin, used later on for the manufacture of porcelain. The tiny pierced lug- and tubular-handles must have served for the suspension of this vessel, witness to the trust their makers had in its solidity. These two vessels made of fundamentally identical material illustrate the technical ability and versatility of the people of this period.

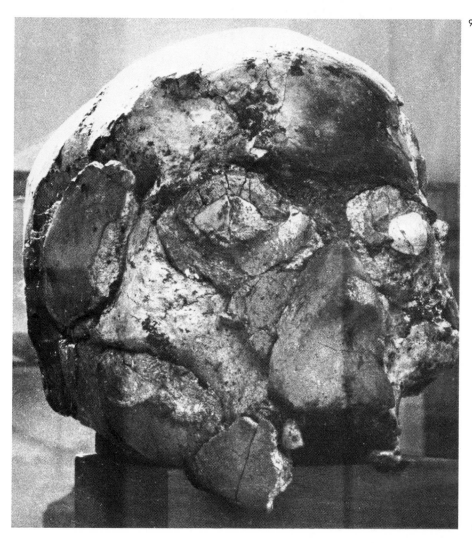

9. Jericho Skull (*c.* 6000 BC)   **(R)**
At Neolithic Jericho human skulls were
found under the floors of the houses, the
features having been recreated in
plaster and painted to resemble flesh,
the eyes indicated by inlaid sea-shells.
The practice of burying skulls under
the living quarters suggests a sort of ancestor-worship, perhaps with the idea of
adding the ancestor's power to that of
the living, maybe also to placate the
deceased.

Aegean, to redistribute them in artifacts made of ivory, clay and
stone, via the Eastern Mediterranean, to North Africa and Spain. We
find their eclectic style carried through to Hellenistic times, when it
was absorbed by strong Western trends. These same trends also
brought coins to these shores, whether early coins of monetary value
from the province of Judah in the Persian Empire or those used
during the Crusades. Some of the rare collections assembled in this
country are shown in the Israel Museum.

When we come to these periods, we again encounter the difficulty
of exhibiting the culture of Judah and Israel in its material aspect.
One cannot demonstrate in any material way the fundamental diff-
erence between early prophets, magicians, those who induced ecstatic
states through ritual nakedness (1 Sam. 19:24) and music (1 Sam.
10:5), and the later prophets, whose main concern was the ethical
precepts of the Law as set against formalized temple service. The
same difficulty is also encountered if one wishes to examine Samuel's
warning to the people who clamoured for a king who would 'Judge
us like all the nations'—that just such a royal rule would eventually
transform a free people into royal servants (1 Sam. 8). The only exhibits which can be shown are, naturally enough, written documents.
The most telling of these is undoubtedly 'the poor man's letter',
addressed to a Royal Governor, which is in stark contrast to the luxury exhibited in the royal citadels of Judah and Israel, a luxury (one

hastens to add) considered normal by all of this strange people's neighbours.

The Period of Destruction, of Return and of Persian overrule (586–332 BC) brings Greek imports to the finds in the country, presaging another wave of western conquest: the Hellenistic period (332–152 BC) which, from the viewpoint of material culture continues into the period of political independence under the Hasmoneans (152–37 BC). It seems a miracle that despite the great influx of Greek culture and language the Jewish ethical code and religious precepts were yet able to survive. From the museum's point of view, the now familiar pattern repeats itself: beside the rich finds of statues, statuettes, and lavishly decorated sarcophagi of the Graeco-Roman world, we have the finds of Jewish houses and tombs of the period, which even when elaboration is the aim, tend to a certain superficiality and lack of finish. It is almost as though one detects here an expression of impatience with material matters, if not a disdain; perhaps a not unnatural attitude for a people at that period more and more occupied with eschatological problems, problems which brought conservative Sadducean land-owners and temple aristocracy into an open clash with Pharisaic artisans and rabbis. This clash comes to a head during the Herodian Period and the times of Roman governorship and destruction (37 BC–AD 70). On the theological level, this dispute is best exemplified by Sadducean rejection of the belief in resurrection, affirmed by the Pharisees; on the political level, by a ditty sung in those days in Jerusalem's streets against the ruling priests, those collaborators of Roman imperialism:

> *Woe is me because of Boethus' House,*
> *Woe is me because of their cudgels!*
> *Woe is me because of Hanin's House,*
> *Woe is me because of their conclaves!*
> *Woe is me because of Kathros' House,*
> *Woe is me because of their writing-reeds!*
> *Woe is me because of Ismael Ben-Phabi's House,*
> *Woe is me because of their fists!*
> > *High Priests are they;*
> > *Treasurers their sons;*
> > *Their sons-in-law trustees;*
> > *And their servants*
> > > *Beat the People with sticks!*

On the fringes of these social and religious disputes we find smaller groups: the Essenes, probably identical with the Qumran Community, who left us the Dead Sea Scrolls; the group of Jesus's Disciples,

10

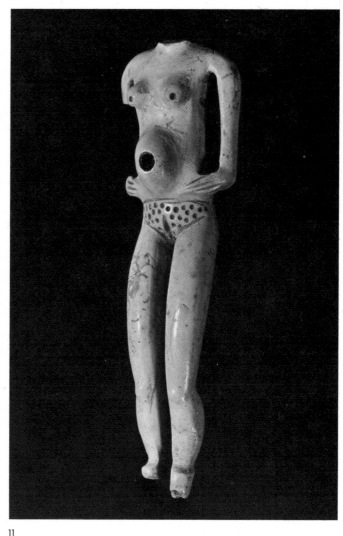

11

10. Horvat Minha Venus (second half of the fifth millennium BC) Horvat Minha, Jordan Valley. Height 0.14 m. clay **(IM)**
While fragments of similar figurines have been found in appropriate archaeological layers both on the sea-shore near Tel Aviv and in the Jordan valley at Sha'ar Ha-Golan, this figurine is the only complete one found in Israel. Like similar figurines from Anatolia, they attest to their significance at a period which saw the beginnings of agriculture—the cultivation of wild grain, wild emmer and wheat and the domestication of animals. It has been suggested that the distribution of food, if not the actual cultivation, was woman's main task, while hunting and trapping remained man's main contribution to the food supplies. It is possible that our figurine thus represents man's earliest deity, the Great Mother.

11. Pregnant Woman (c. 3500 BC) Beersheba. Height 0.11 m. ivory **(IM)**
This very delicate figurine is one of a group carved from African elephant tusks by local inhabitants, whose ancestors may have come from the north-eastern borders of the Syrian desert about 4000 BC, bringing with them domesticated sheep. They demonstrate a great technical ability and a true artistic sensibility in all media at their disposal: clay, ivory, copper, basketry and woven material. As to the significance of this particular figurine, and others which show pronouncedly male characteristics, it seems reasonable to assume that they had some religious or magical purpose connected with fertility.

known after his death as *Evyonim* (Ebionites, the Poor Ones); the Zealots, devoted Freedom Fighters against Rome, and their radical wing, the Siccarians, so named after the dagger they carried—and used for political murder. After the inevitable clash between them and Rome, and the latter's inevitable victory (though at a high price in casualties), we encounter one additional group of Jewish Freedom Fighters succumbing to Rome's might in AD 135—the troops of Shim'on Bar Koseva who, until the discovery of his district commander's letters in a cave above En Gedi, had been a rather shadowy legendary figure; even his name was disputed, being interpreted by his followers as Bar Kokhba ('Star's Son' or Messiah), and by his detractors as Bar Kozivah (from *kazav*, a lie), 'Son of Falsehood'. These letters, and parts of the Dead Sea Scrolls, are exhibited in the **Shrine of the Book**. In addition, through the private records of a woman named Babata, who took refuge in the same cave, there is a clear account of financial and domestic affairs of the day. Items of daily use—including a small boy's jerkin, and the lady's keys, mirror and wool—give us a vivid picture of the eternal hope of refugees, though only their belongings and their bones remain to tell the tale.

While statehood was thus lost to the people, together with the temple and its service, a new receptacle for Israel's spirit had been created: the synagogue, house of reading and interpretation of the Law, birthplace of an unending dialectical process between teacher and disciple, between sages of every successive generation; to be eventually continued in prayer as an endless dialogue between man and God, carried along in the unbroken chain of everyday dealings.

Out of the institution of the Synagogue, already established while the Temple still stood, the Christian Church was to emerge, many of its institutions and ethics being similar, but their fundamental religious thought diverging sharply, right from the beginning. Perhaps this divergence is expressed best by their two symbols: the seven-branched candelabra, the Menorah, which was interpreted as the symbol of eternal, living and divine light, brought to earth in the days of creation, to be re-absorbed into the Godhead at the end of Days; and the Cross, symbol of death and resurrection, taken by the Godhead upon itself for the redemption of mankind, who would accept this sacrifice in order to be redeemed through faith.

At a more material level, it can be seen how the same groups of craftsmen, working with pattern-books, satisfied customers of both religions with similar mosaic floors, sarcophagi, lamps, even amulets against the evil eye, inserting or superimposing the symbols of faith appropriate to the prospective customer. With the Arab conquest in AD 640 we find a new religion emerging from the desert, influenced

12. a–b. Ibex 'Sceptre and Crown'
(*c.* 3500 BC) Nahal Mishmar. Height
0.275 and 0.175 m. copper **(IM)**
The cave where these items come from is
situated high up the cliff of Nahal Mishmar, a gorge of the Judaean desert,
opening up towards En Gedi. At that
latter place, near its spring, is a contemporary sanctuary which originally
may have contained these artifacts, together with 427 other items, most of
copper and some of elephant and hippo
ivory. The treasure was found in the
cave, wrapped in a straw mat. The
workmanship of the copper utensils,
cast in the lost wax process, is highly
sophisticated; indeed it reveals another
aspect of the great technical and artistic
skills of man at this period. Though the
exact use of these and other items in the
treasure have not been established, they
seem to have been used in religious
ceremonials, perhaps at the sanctuary
mentioned above.

by both its predecessors: Islam, propagating the belief in one compassionate God, to be worshipped through prayer, good deeds, pilgrimage—and the sword. The new religion left buildings and writings, and in its early period—strangely enough for such an iconoclastic creed—left also its statues, reliefs, and wall-paintings, lingering influences from the West, to be slowly re-absorbed in the East's arabesques. The sweep of their conquest over the shores of Israel towards Asia Minor, North Africa and into Europe, was eventually met by a Western counter-wave, known in history as the Crusades, which succeeded in implanting for a while a Romanesque culture upon these shores between 1099 and 1291. This culture often absorbed Oriental influences locally, eventually being taken back to Europe, while these same Oriental trends formalized on the shores of the Eastern Mediterranean, finally becoming repetitious and stagnant.

A special section of the **Biblical and Archaeological Museum** is dedicated to the neighbouring ancient cultures, comprising fine examples of antiquities from this part of the world. **The Bezalel Museum** follows the cultural history of the Jewish People into the Diaspora. It has one of the largest collections of Jewish ceremonial art and an important group of Hebrew illuminated manuscripts. A beautiful cross-section of the latter is on permanent exhibition, arranged so as to enable the visitor to see all aspects of the Diaspora through all periods, from the presentation of the Shabbat to that of the feast-days of the year; and onward to the rites-of-passage of the individual Jew's life: birth, coming-of-age, marriage, death. The main lesson emerging from this exhibition is the manifest readiness of the Jewish people to absorb the style and artistic expression of the land and the period in which it found itself, so that local fashions influenced objects used for religious, communal, and private use. Clothes, too, are displayed here in an impressive array.

13. Fish-shaped Vessels (*c.* 1700–1550 BC) **(IM)**
The alabaster vessel on the left comes from Tell al-Ajjul, between Gaza and Ashkelon. The one on the right (0.18 m. in length) is from Tell Poleg in the Sharon plain, and is of so-called Tell al-Yahudiyya ware, after the place in Egypt where it was first discovered. Pottery of this type, mainly juglets, characterized by a blackish clay almost covered in an incised and punctured decoration filled with white chalk, has been discovered in local excavations, in one case in a kiln, as yet unbaked. There may exist some connection between the Hyksos, ruling at this period both Egypt and Canaan, and this particular type of ware. Zoomorphic vessels were at this time especially popular, both here and in neighbouring countries.

14

14. Animal Figurine (3100–2900 BC) Bet Yerah. Length 0.053 m. clay **(R)** Animal figures of this period of transition from the Chalcolithic to the early Canaanite age, have been variously interpreted as either representing cattle or dogs. The purpose of their manufacture is also in dispute; they may have been intended as votive offerings, or simply as children's toys. What is not in dispute is the artistic skill that managed to create, from a tiny mud pellet, the spirited representation of an animal.

It is interesting to observe the many styles in which the Torah, the scroll of the Law, was adorned; to see, side by side, European baroque and Oriental arabesque; and at the same time to observe how very painstakingly the ancient Jewish regulations were observed in the actual writing of the scroll and in the preparation of the ink and the parchment, the number of lines in the column, the number of letters in the line—and that equally in all parts of the Diaspora. It goes without saying that the text was transferred from generation to generation without the slightest change. This preoccupation with the written word, and the ideas it expressed, seems to have gone hand in hand with a certain indifference to form and style, which were regarded as essentially a temporal and perishable shell. The main interest of the people remains concentrated in the ideas and values embodied in the Torah.

The fine arts division of the museum exhibits a small but choice collection of European paintings, graphics and sculpture, from the fifteenth century to recent times, including major works by great artists. It must be borne in mind that no original European art was executed in Israel later than the Crusader period, and of that very little remains. This lack is keenly felt by the public, both permanent and special exhibitions of such art drawing large numbers of visitors. A large part of Picasso's graphic work is included in the well-endowed graphics study-room, while a special pavilion for design has been recently added to the museum. A start has been made on the creation of further rooms such as the very fine eighteenth-century one, originally in the Hôtel Samuel Bernard in the Faubourg Saint-Germain, Paris, reconstructed in the museum.

The Sculpture Garden to the west of the museum, designed by Isamu Noguchi, has a pavilion containing about one hundred and thirty sculptural pieces by Lipchitz, also fine examples of modern sculpture, ranging from Rodin and Maillol to Picasso and Moore. A special section of the museum is dedicated to modern Israeli art, including paintings, graphics and large sculptures.

The Youth Wing, at present being enlarged, conducts guided tours for groups of young visitors, and has an extensive scheme of afternoon activities within the museum. There is a similar programme at the Rockefeller Museum for young people living in the eastern and north-eastern quarters of the city. Special programmes cover adult activities, and teacher-training courses are given to students in co-operation with the Department of Education of the Hebrew University. For the public at large the Israel museums hold a wide range of lecture programmes, special exhibitions and art film club activities.

15. Bichrome Jug (1550–1400 BC) Tell al-Ajjul. Height 0.31 m. pottery (**R**) This jug belongs to a group of vessels decorated with birds, fishes and other animals, at first ascribed to an Ajjul painter and named after the place of their discovery. In fact, they should be ascribed to a school of potters and painters working along the Canaanite coast, probably originating in the north and towards Syria. Those northern cities, with their rich and eclectic merchants' culture were under Cypriot influence, as is proved by the theme of birds and fishes, a motif preferred there.

16

16. The Lachish Ewer (thirteenth century BC) Lachish. Height 0.45 m. pottery **(R)**
Above the painted decoration of stags flanking a tree of life, runs an inscription in Proto-Canaanite characters (see pl. 19). This inscription runs from left to right and reads in translation: 'Mattan. An offering to my Lady Elat'; it thus seems to be an offering to the shrine of Elat (i.e. 'the Goddess') at Lachish, given by someone named Mattan.

17. Victory Stele of Seti I (1318–1304 BC) Beth Shean. Height 2.46 m. basalt **(R)**
The upper part of the stele shows Seti I making offerings in front of the Egyptian god, Re. Above are the emblems and title of Behudet, the god of Edfu in Upper Egypt. The hieroglyphic inscription below records the repulsion of invaders from Transjordan who had attacked the city of Beth Shean with three Egyptian army divisions in a one-day battle.

18. Statue of Ramses III (1196–1166 BC) Beth Shean. Height 1.50 m. basalt (*overleaf*) **(R)**
The pharaoh here shown engaged in pitched battles with the 'sea-peoples'—Philistines and other tribes who came from Asia Minor, the Greek mainland and the Aegean Islands, having fought their way through the Hittite Empire, attacking the Egyptians on land and sea. This statue thus marks the end of Egyptian rule over the Asiatic bridge-head.

I. **'Ashoda',** early twelfth century BC. The Israel Museum, Jerusalem. (Note 34)

II. **The Dancers' Jar,** Wilfrid Israel House, Hazorea. (Note 279)

III. **Gold glass,** first half of fourth century AD. The Israel Museum, Jerusalem. (Note 56)

IV. **Egyptian Couple,** *c.* 1425 BC. The Israel Museum, Jerusalem. (Note 65)

V. **The Horb Synagogue Ceiling,** 1735. The Israel Museum, Jerusalem. (Note 79)

VI. **Hallah Cover,** nineteenth century. The Israel Museum, Jerusalem. (Note 78)

VII. **Arab Woman's Jewellery,** late tenth century. The Israel Museum, Jerusalem. (Note 61)

VIII. **Yemenite Bride,** recent. The Israel Museum, Jerusalem. (Note 82)

IX. **Jacob Gerritz and Albert Cuyp,** *The Return from the Hunt*, 1641. The Israel Museum, Jerusalem. (Note 84)

X. **Paul Cézanne,** *Country House by the Riverside,* 1888–90. The Israel Museum, Jerusalem. (Note 90)

19. Proto-Canaanite Inscription (*c.* 1600 BC) Gezer.
Height 0.07 m. pottery **(R)**
This sherd, originally part of an offering stand, was found
accidentally on the ancient site of Gezer in 1929. The signs
incised on it are considered to be the earliest Proto-Canaanite
inscription known to date. It has tentatively been read—
starting from above—as K L B, perhaps spelling out the
Semitic name Caleb. The alphabetic script, giving the value
of the initial letter of the Semitic word to drawings of the
appropriate item, caught on quickly. In this case, the upper
letter K stands for *Kaph*—hand, the lower—B—for *Bayt*,
house. Consonants only were used; the vowels are missing.
So-called Proto-Sinaitic inscriptions, found in mines operated
for the Egyptians by Semitic miners from the fifteenth
century BC onwards, must be considered a branch of this
script, which was used down to the twelfth century BC, to be
slowly replaced by Phoenician script in the eleventh century
BC and by Hebrew either in the twelfth or eleventh centuries
BC. Eventually this script found its way to the Greeks, who
turned its letters to face from left to right, preferring this as
the direction of their writing. Thus it became the prototype
of the Roman alphabet and subsequently of all Western
alphabets.

20

21

20. Mekal Stele (fourteenth century BC) Beth Shean. Height 0.28 m. limestone   **(R)**
This small stele comes from a temple in Beth Shean, at the height of Egyptian imperial rule. To the right are shown the dedicators, the Egyptian architect Amen-em-Opet and his son, worshipping the god who is enthroned in Egyptian fashion on the left. This god, is, however, identified as a local Canaanite deity by his horned conical cap and his pointed beard, as well as in the dedicatory inscription, which identifies him, albeit in Egyptian hieroglyphics, by his Semitic name and title, 'Mekal, Baal Beth Shean'—Mekal, the Lord of Beth Shean. The religious syncretism, so well exemplified here, has worked in both directions: whenever a conquering army occupied countries with a long religious tradition, its members would placate the local deities, officially or unofficially, in a form usual to their own home-land; moreover they would often take these local deities to their further stations, and eventually to their own lands.

21. Head of Hathor (mid-thirteenth century BC) Beth Shean. Height 0.10 m. bronze and gold foil   **(R)**
The bronze, its face originally entirely covered with gold foil, is complete. It was once attached to some wooden object, probably as the emblem on top of a standard. It represents the Egyptian goddess Hathor, crowned with lunar disk and cow-horns, the royal uraeus on her forehead. It was found in a temple, much resembling the royal chapels of Akhenaton at Tell el-Amarna.

22. Canaanite Gold Jewellery (1550–1300 BC)   **(R)**
Most of the jewellery shown here comes from Tell al-Ajjul, at that period an important harbour-town between Gaza and Ashkelon. However, the small pendant (centre left) showing an Egyptian goddess, and the toggle-pin (right, length 0.08 m.), come from Beth Shean. The latter was for a long period—the seventeenth to the twelfth centuries BC—the main method of fastening a garment. The amulet to the upper left combines the form of a flying hawk, an Egyptian motif with the shape of a local plant's seed pods. It is made in granulated work, which was invented at that time and can still be seen in modern jewellery: small gold pellets, fashioned with the blow-pipe on glowing charcoal, being soldered to the gold base to produce the desired pattern. Both the central and the lower right pendants are made in *repoussé*—i.e. the decoration is punched from the back. The central pendant represents a local goddess of fertility, though the face shows Egyptian characteristics. The emphasis on the stylized sexual organs is Canaanite. The flies and the bee pendants on the lower left may be amulets. It has been suggested that the former may be connected with a Canaanite god, called in the Bible *Baal Zevuv*—Baal Zebub, 'Lord of Flies'—eventually becoming in modern usage a devil named Beelzebub. It seems more likely, however, that this god's name was originally *Baal-Zevul*, 'Lord of the Prince'; in fact we find his name still written in this manner in the New Testament's Greek version, while Hebrew and later versions changed his name in mockery. Thus our little amulets may simply have been intended to keep away flies and wild bees, both a very real nuisance on a hot day in the open country or in the markets of a populated city.

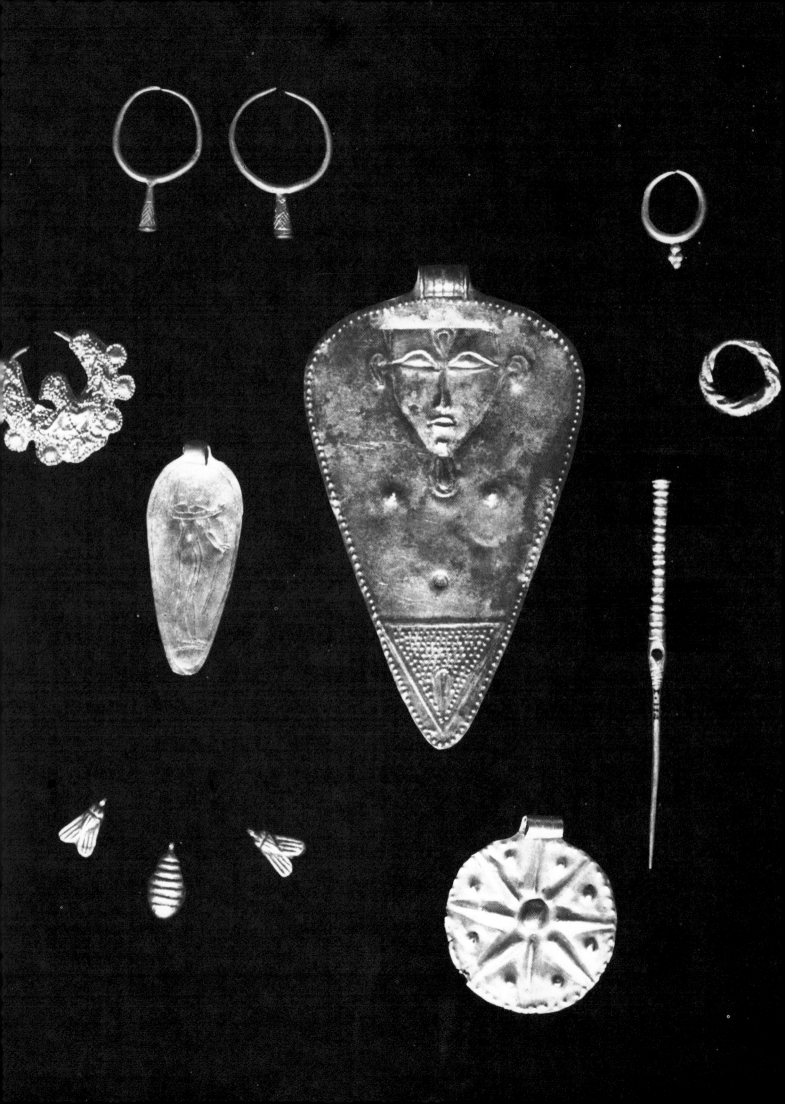

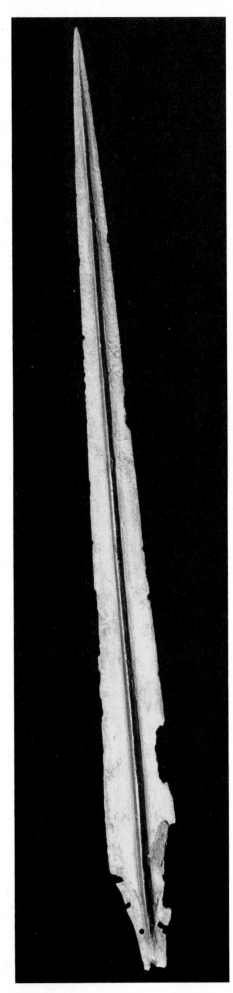

24

23. Philistine Sword (first quarter of eleventh century BC) unknown provenance. Length 1.55 m. bronze **(R)** This long bronze sword resembles the swords carried by Philistines and other 'sea-peoples' in representations of their battles with the army and navy of Ramses III (1192–1160 BC). It is a most efficient thrusting and cutting weapon, characterized by a central ridge and a keenly honed blade, tapering off to the sharp point.

24. Orthostat (*c.* 1400 BC) Beth Shean. Height 0.89 m. basalt. **(R)** This slab was not found in its original archaeological layer. It must have belonged to some temple of the Late Canaanite period and seems to be of Syro-Hittite workmanship. The subject is in dispute: most experts see in it a representation of the fight between lions and mastifs, perhaps with some symbolic meaning (for Syro-Hittite connections see also the Hazor finds, pls. 261–3).

23

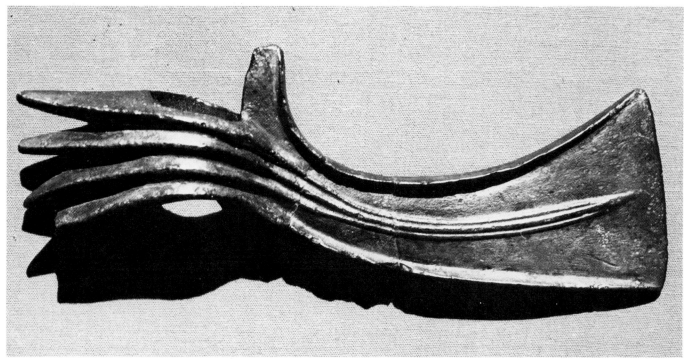

25

26

25. Hittite Axe (fourteenth century BC) Beth Shean. Length 0.19 m. bronze
(R)
The part opposite the blade seems to represent an outstretched hand. A similar axe is carried by a Hittite king on a relief from the King's Gate at Boghazköy, the ancient capital of the Hittites in Asia Minor. It may serve as a good example of the connections between that country and the North.

26. Seated God (eleventh century BC) Hazor. Height 0.13 m. bronze **(IM)**
The head of this figurine which must have originally held some weapon in its left hand, bears a conical helmet. It was found under a temple, antedating the Solomonic city, together with a sword, javelin, arrow-heads, and an axe—seemingly the foundation offering of some warrior. This representation of a warrior-god continues a Late Canaanite tradition.

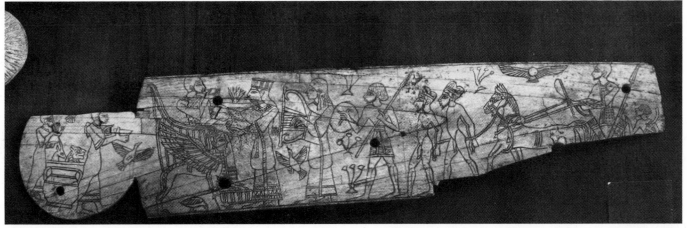

28

29

27. Lid of Anthropoid Sarcophagus
(twelfth century BC) Beth Shean. Height
0.63 m. pottery (**IM**)
Both at Beth Shean and on the southern
sea-coast of Israel, jar-shaped sarcophagi
have been discovered, the lid representing the upper part of the deceased's
body. While this is clearly a contemporary Egyptian practice, the Beth
Shean group is singled out by the
strongly emphasized features: narrow
lips, the straight line of the nose continued by the straight eyebrows, and a
head-dress characteristic of some of the
'sea-peoples' as they appear on the
reliefs of Ramses III, who first fought
them, and later employed some of them
in his garrison at Beth Shean. Eventually they replaced Egyptian rule, especially along the southern and central
part of the sea-coast. One of these
peoples—the Philistines—finally left
their name to the country for long
stretches of its history—i.e. Palestine.

28. A Canaanite King's Triumph
(c. 1200 BC) Megiddo. Length 0.26 m.
ivory, engraved (**R**)
The king is represented twice. To the
right, he returns from battle in his
chariot, the royal winged sun-disk over
his head; he is followed by his steward
who carries a sickle-sword, and is pre-
ceded by a soldier and two captives, one
circumcised, tied to his chariot. To the
left, the king celebrates his victory,
seated on a throne which has cherubim
as its sides (cf. Ps. 99:1). He is attended
by his wife and a female lyre-player;
behind him are his servants, preparing
more drink, some of which the king will
receive from rhytons in the shape of
animal heads. The plaque was probably
attached with pegs to a wooden box.

29. Mycenaean and Cypriot Imports
(fourteenth century BC) (**IM**)
The Mycenaean jar to the left comes
from a tomb at Gezer; its height is 0.17
m.; the beautiful cylix nearby, the jug
and the bowl (height 0.06 m.) are
Cypriot, as is the little bull-shaped
vessel in the foreground. While the
latter was found at Bahan, in the
Sharon plain, the three former are part
of a group of fifty-six vessels, many of
them imported, found in a tomb in
Jerusalem. Jerusalem was then off the
main highways; however it has been
pointed out that the Amarna letters,
discovered in Egypt (a diplomatic cor-
respondence written by the local city-
kings to the pharaoh), refer to an alliance
at that period between the king of Jerusalem and the kings of Acre and Ach-
shaph; such affluent imports were then
common on the country's coast.

47

30

30. Gold Ring (end of second century AD) Caesarea. Diam.
0.025 m. gold **(IM)**
The device on the bezel shows the Tyche—personification of
the city—of Caesarea, flanked by a trophy and a statue of
Victory, standing on a column and presenting a crown to the
city. The name of the ring's owner, inscribed below, is rather
surprising: Ampelis means 'young vine' and was the pro-
fessional name of a hetaira. It is referred to in Lucian's
writings, contemporary to the ring.

31

31. Nemesis' Griffin (210 AD) Erez. Height 0.48 m.
marble **(IM)**
This winged griffin was conceived as associate of Nemesis,
the Greek goddess of vengeance. It is shown here with its
attribute, the wheel of Destiny. A Greek inscription on its
pedestal gives the exact date of its dedication.

32

32. The Poor Man's Letter (late-seventh century BC) Mesad Hashavyahu. Height 0.21 m. ostracon (ink on potsherd) **(IM)**
This letter was found in the guard-room of an excavated Judaean fortress half-way between Jaffa and Ashdod. The letter is written in Hebrew as dictated by a petitioner and is addressed to the local governor who administered the coastal plain for King Josiah of Judah (640–609 BC). The petitioner is a reaper, who seems to have formed part of a group of corvée-labourers, working on the royal estates (see pl. 35). The discrepancy between the scribe's opening formula and the repetitive style of the reaper, unsure of the 'proper' mode of address, is most revealing of the latter's humble estate as well as of his real anguish at having been deprived of his single upper garment, the only cover against the sun's heat at work in the field, and against the night's cold at his rest. The letter reads: 'Let my lord the governor hear the word of his servant! Thy servant was reaping, thy servant in Haser-Asam. Thy servant reaped and finished and gathered as usual. Before the rest, when thy servant had finished his reaping, and gathered as usual, Hoshaiahu son of Shobai came and took thy servant's garment. When I had already finished this my reaping as usual, Hoshaiahu took thy servant's garment. And all my brethren will answer for me, those who reap with me in the heat of the sun. My brethren will answer for me. Amen. I am absolved of guilt. Please return my garment, and I shall deliver it in full. The governor should return the garment of thy servant and grant him mercy. Let thy servant's garment be returned and do not dismiss him . . .' The plaintive words clearly echo the Lord's command as formulated in the Jewish Biblical Law: 'If thou at all take thy neighbour's raiment to pledge, thou shalt deliver it unto him by that the sun goeth down: For that is his covering only, it is his raiment for his skin: wherein shall he sleep? And it shall come to pass, when he crieth unto me, that I will hear; for I am gracious.' It was the disregard of such fundamental laws which provoked the harsh prophesies of Jeremiah against the ruling class of Judah, foreseeing the inevitable punishment. The letter seems never to have reached the governor and most probably went unheeded. The fortress fell in 609 BC to Pharaoh Neco. Twenty-three years later Jerusalem's first temple was burned by Nebuchadnezzar and its king taken into captivity.

33. Holy of Holies (ninth century BC) Arad. Base dimensions: 2.2 × 1.6 m. stone **(IM)**

The excavations at Arad on the southern fringe of the Judaean hills uncovered a local temple similar in lay-out to the Temple in Jerusalem. It has the identical tripartite division into Porch, Main Hall and Holy of Holies; the latter, transferred to Jerusalem, is shown here. It includes two altars, both of which still hold the remnants of the last incense offering, and an upright stone which represents the male deity. It is possible that this temple was destroyed under King Josiah of Judah (640–609 BC), who aimed at a complete centralization of religious worship in Jerusalem.

34. *Colour plate I.* **'Ashdoda'** (early twelfth century BC) Ashdod. Height 0.17 m. terra cotta **(IM)**

This figurine is a schematic combination of woman and throne. Its painted decoration marks it as Philistine, of a type derived from representations of the Great Mother, goddess of the Mycenaean world. It is so far the only figurine of its kind to have been found complete in Israel, though many fragments of other similar ones were discovered in the Ashdod excavations. This is a proof that the great deity was worshipped amongst the Philistines, and a further indication of their Aegean cultural background.

33

35

35. Palace Balustrade (seventh century BC) Ramat Rahel. Height 0.36 m. stone **(IM)**
The fragments of this balustrade were found in the excavation of a royal palace on a hill south of Jerusalem. They still show traces of red paint. Though this is local Judaean work the style is Phoenician, as proven by the adjacent ivory from Nimrod, of the end of the ninth century BC, shown in the much enlarged photo. Phoenician style and craftsmanship had already been introduced into Israel by itinerant artisans of that versatile people under King Solomon (*cf.* 1 K.5; 1 K. 7:13 f.). The sumptuous style of such a royal house, with its ivory-inlaid furniture, was frowned upon by the prophets (*cf.* Amos 6:4). The Ramat Rahel palace may indeed be the palace which gave rise to Jeremiah's anger against King Jehoiakim (668–597 BC): 'Woe unto him that buildeth his house by unrighteousness, and his chambers by wrong; that useth his neighbour's service without wages, and giveth him not for his work. That saith: I will build me a wide house and large chambers, and cutteth him out windows; and it is ceiled with cedar, and painted with vermilion' (22:13).

36

36. Hebrew Official's Seal (late seventh century BC) Mizpah. Length 0.02 m. onyx **(R)**
The inscription reads: '(Belonging) to Jaazaniahu/Servant of the King.' Many seals of royal officials have by now come to light. They were used for official business in the King's name and were carried as his token of authority. 'Servant' (*ebed*) was obviously a high title, as was 'scribe' (*sopher*), 'squire' (*na'ar*) and others which appear on such seals. The fighting cock seems to be a family crest. Further crests of this character have been found on Hebrew seals.

37

38

37. Jerusalem Inscription (701 BC)
Amazyah. Height 0.65 m. stone (IM)
The inscription, discovered in the entrance-chamber of a tomb, was scratched on a wall. It reads in part 'YHWE is the God of the whole earth; the mountains of Judah belong to him, to the God of Jerusalem'. This and some other graffiti, expressing defiance of an invader and trust in the Lord, seem to have been incised by some refugees from one of the cities of Judah, captured by the Babylonians under Sennacherib in 701 BC. This inscription contains the earliest known mention of Jerusalem in an original ancient Hebrew text.

38. Pregnant Woman (sixth to fifth centuries BC) Achzib. Height 0.22 m. terra cotta (IM)
This very fine and sensitive representation of a seated pregnant woman is one of many mould-made Phoenician figurines, appearing wherever this industrious people had its cities and colonies, all along the Mediterranean shore. Their mixed style is expressed here by an Egyptian head-dress worn by a local woman. It seems likely that such figurines also had some magical function, perhaps ensuring fecundity, or easing labour in child-birth. It is, however, curious to find them fairly often in tombs, where personal belongings, food and drink, are witnesses to the belief in some form of life in the netherworld. (See also pl. 188.)

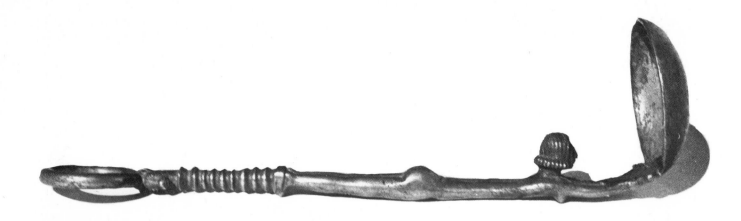

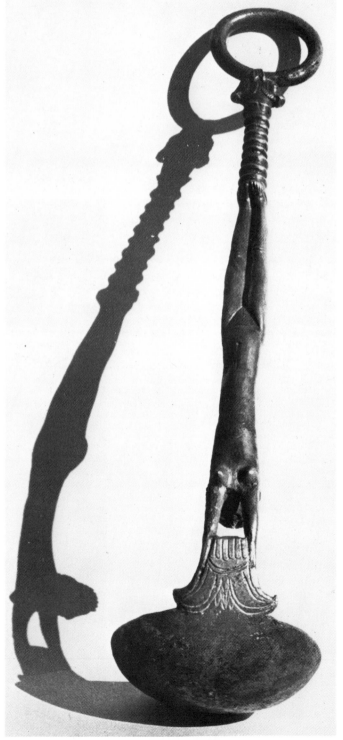

39

39. Bathing Woman (seventh century BC) Achzib. Height
0.18 m. terracotta   (**R**)
This lively figurine of a woman at her bath was found in one
of Achzib's many Phoenician tombs. It is possible that it was
put there to give to those in the netherworld some of the
pleasures of the living. The Aegean world does indeed know
baths from much earlier times. Both there and in the Near
and Middle East, these were used at times, significantly
enough, as coffins.

40. Phoenician Ladle (fifth century BC) Tell el Far'ah.
Length 0.22 m. silver   (**R**)
This graceful ladle was found in a tomb of some wealthy local
man, living at ancient Sharuhen during the rule of the
Persian Empire. He was buried on his wooden couch with
precious silver objects at his side. These include the ladle
shown here, fashioned in a remarkable manner. The naked,
fully-stretched girl forming the ladle's handle is an ancient
Egyptian motif, while the pair of animal heads which flank
the elaborately turned column, similar to throne legs, are
both Persian motifs. A Phoenician lotus connects the handle
to the bowl, while the girl's features are local. In short, this is
a classic example of the continuation of the eclectic Phoenician style.

41

42

41. Jewish Sarcophagus and Ossuaries (mid-first century BC to AD 135) Jerusalem. Limestone **(IM)**
In the background a life-size photograph shows the inside of a characteristic loculi-tomb of the period's Jewish necropolis of Jerusalem. The sarcophagus exhibited at the back, richly adorned with garlands and clusters of grapes in relief, belonged to the wife of a very wealthy citizen, himself buried in the same vault built of ashlars, in a plain sarcophagus. Both he and his father are identified as Nazarites—that is, people who vowed to abstain from wine and from cutting their hair. The ossuaries exhibited are small stone receptacles used for the collection of the deceased's bones after the flesh had decayed. This peculiar custom existed amongst Jews for a very short time from about the forties of the first century BC. It seems to have originated in Pharisaic circles in Jerusalem, who then considered, in explicit opposition to the Sadducees, personal bodily resurrection to be part of the Jewish creed. The wish to assure expiation of 'fleshly' sins after the decay of the flesh, and then to preserve the individual's bones for his resurrection both seem to have been the cause of this custom, which disappeared in the beginning of the third century AD, when more spiritual concepts of after-life prevailed.

42. Yehud Coin (fourth century BC) Israel. Diam. 0.008 m. silver **(IM)**
This is an exceptional specimen of the minute silver coins which Persian rulers permitted the local governors of Judah to mint. On its obverse side this coin carries the falcon and the Hebrew inscription 'Yehud', i.e. Judah, and the fleur-de-lis of Jerusalem on its reverse. Another type, more common, uses the Athenian device of the owl, and carries in Hebrew the name of Hezekiah, and his official title, *Hapeha* (Governor) (*cf.* Neh. 12:26).

43. Ephesian Artemis (second century AD) Caesarea. Height 1.90 m. marble **(IM)**

The statue, discovered in excavations at Caesarea, capital of the Roman province of Syria-Palaestina, is evidence enough of this goddess's great popularity at the time. We have here one of many contemporary copies of the famous cult-statue of this mountain goddess of Asia Minor, identified at Ephesus with the classic Greek goddess Artemis, light-footed virgin huntress, ranging the woods with her hounds and nymphs, identified by the Romans as Diana.

It is interesting to observe the way in which the Oriental execution has absorbed this concept in the formalized image of the goddess, ensconced in a stiff sheath covered with symbolic animals, hung with fertility symbols, far removed from its free western image.

44. Hazor Citadel's Gate (ninth to eighth centuries BC) Height 3.20 m. stone **(IM)**
We see a reconstructed entrance-gate from Hazor's royal citadel. The so-called Proto-Aeolic capitals are, together with the mason's skill and the careful execution of the builder's work, an Israelite absorption of Phoenician techniques learned by their forebears from the master-craftsmen sent out from Tyre in the days of King Solomon (see I K. 5–7).

45. Dedicatory Inscription of Pontius Pilate (AD 26–36) Caesarea. Height 0.80 m. limestone **(IM)**
This Latin inscription, which reads: '. . STIBERIEVM . . PON TIVSPILATVS . . . PRAEF ECTVSIVDA EA E', should be restored to read: 'The Prefect of Judaea Pontius Pilate erected the Tiberieum in honour of Tiberius Caesar'. Outside the scriptures this is the only reference to the Roman prefect (not procurator, as tradition styles him) who had crucified Jesus.

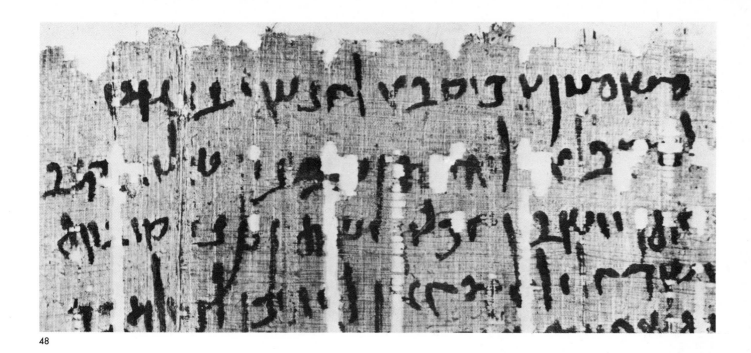

48

46. The Theodotos Synagogue Inscription (Herodian period—prior to AD 70) Jerusalem. Height 0.42 m. limestone **(R)**
This inscription, found in 1914 in excavations on the south-eastern slope of Jerusalem's Temple Mount ('the City of David'), is so far the only remnant of four hundred and eighty synagogues said to have stood in Jerusalem before the destruction of the Second Temple in AD 70. It is in Greek, though it mentions a Jewish family with the Roman name Vetinus. Its text, which lists all the functions of any present-day synagogue (except for communal prayer, which was introduced to replace the offerings in the Temple, after the latter's destruction), reads in translation: 'Theodotos son of [or, of the family of] Vettenos, priest and head of the synagogue, son of the head of the synagogue, who was also the son of the head of the synagogue, [re]built the synagogue for the reading of the Law and for the study of the precepts, as well as the hospice and the chambers and the bathing-establishment, for lodging those who need them, from abroad; it [the synagogue] was founded by his ancestors and the elders and the Simonides.'

47. The Isaiah Scroll (100 BC) Qumran Caves. Height 0.26 m. leather **(IM)**
A Jewish sect, presumably the Essenes, living in an isolated community at the north-west corner of the Dead Sea, hid their sacred books in about AD 68 inside specially prepared pottery-jars, in a number of caves above their settlement. These documents, written between the second half of the second century BC and AD 68, comprise books of the Bible-canon and sectarian writings. The latter include commentaries to books of the Bible, rules and regulations of the sect and details of their religious concepts as well as their own psalms.

The large Isaiah scroll, with all sixty-six chapters of the book, is 7.35 metres long, the accurately prepared sheets of leather carefully sewn one to another. It is, in fact, the oldest Biblical manuscript so far discovered, having been written some one hundred and sixty years before it was hidden away. Despite its long use, the writing is in a clear Hebrew hand, legible to anyone versed in the language, as vivid as the words here reproduced, containing Isaiah 49:2 to 52:12, meaningful in our days to Jew and Christian alike, each according to his own religious concept.

48. Bar Kokhba's Letter (AD 135) Judaean desert. Width 0.09 m. papyrus (*above*) **(IM)**
The cave above En Gedi, on the western shore of the Dead Sea, in which this letter was found, is now named 'the Cave of the Letters'. It is situated high up on the side of a steep cliff of the Judaean hills, overlooking the Dead Sea. Here, as often in the previous history of this region, some of these caves served as a last refuge for freedom-fighters, in this case the local commanders, some of their men and some civilians from En Gedi, who formed part of the troups of Bar Kokhba in the second war of the Jews against Rome (AD 132–135). The cave yielded the personal belongings and documents of a rich woman of En Gedi, Roman bronze vessels, perhaps taken in a desperate sortie from a detachment of the Roman legion camping above the cave, the reburied remains of the refugees—mostly children and women—perhaps interred in the cave by some pious hand several years after their dying from hunger and thirst, and the military archives of the local commanders, containing letters from their commander-in-chief, Shim'on Bar Koseva. Until the discovery of his letters, this commander had been only a legendary figure, even his name being in doubt and interpreted in various allegorical ways. In the letters, however, we not only have his full name and title, but also something of his personality: ardent, pious, taciturn and harsh. One of his letters is reproduced here. Written in cursive Hebrew, the opening sentences read: 'From Shim'on bar Koseva to the people of En Gedi ... In comfort you sit, eat and drink from the property of the House of Israel and care nothing for your brothers ...'

49

50

49. Roman Altar (218–19 AD) Al-Lajjun. Height 1.05 m. marble **(R)**

This marble altar comes from ancient Legio, centre of the Legio VI Ferrata (the 'Iron' Legion), which was added to Roman forces in Syria-Palaestina after their victory over the Jews in 135 AD, and which from then on policed the north of the country. The altar still carries on its top the rust-marks of an iron libation bowl. It is decorated around its drum with two panels showing the Roman legionary eagles, flanking a panel with the personification of Victory, carrying a wreath and a trophy. The much-defaced inscription round the upper edge of the altar seems to have been part of the acclamation sung by Senate and people at the accession of a new emperor. The main inscription on the altar's side is a supplication to Serapis, the Egyptian-Hellenistic god widely worshipped in the Roman Empire, in favour of the Emperor of Syrian descent, Heliogabalus. The altar was erected by the VIth legion and by one Isidorianus (by his name, probably an Egyptian), chief centurion of one of the Legion's divisions. It must have been dedicated at the occasion of Heliogabalus' visit to this part of the Empire; the names referring to him were, however, erased after his fall, by special decree of the Senate.

50. The Avdat Panther (first century AD) Avdat. Height 0.05 m. bronze **(IM)**

This small figure, with black inlays marking the panther's spots, was found together with other small bronzes at Avdat; all of them seem to be very fine copies of Alexandrian originals. These rarities serve as witnesses to the prosperity of the caravan-cities of the Nabateans, Arab conquerors of the Edomites, who had established their rule at the ancient centre of Sela-Edom, eventually called Petra. In the first century BC their rule extended deep into the Negev, reaching, via their cities Shivtah and Avdat, towards the coast. Over their roads from South Arabia to Gaza they transported incense, myrrh and frankincense, indispensable for any temple service of antiquity. With the beginning of the second century AD, however, their land became a province of the Roman Empire and they thus lost their lucrative monopoly.

51

52

51. Portrait Head of a Woman (middle of second century AD) Israel. Height 0.32 m. marble **(R)**
This very fine portrait head, said to come from the Jordan valley, originally seems to have been prepared for insertion in a statue. Eyes and lids are emphasized with colour, as were also the lips and eyebrows. The elaborate hairdo is characteristic of portrait-heads of Roman women under the rule of the Emperors, from Trajan to the early Antonines and should probably be assigned to the latter, i.e., about AD 130 to 140. Some of the realistic Roman portraits were intended for funeral purposes, to be placed in niches in the antechamber of the tomb, but in many cases such portraits were kept in the home.

52. The Good Shepherd (fourth century AD) Gaza district. Height 0.63 m. marble **(R)**
The concept of the deity as a good shepherd goes back to pre-Christian times; in Judaism to the prophets (*cf.* Ezek. 34); in the Greek world to Hermes Kriophoros at Tanagra, while later representations go back to Roman times. Christianity, however, saw this image as the first and foremost representation of the Saviour, in accordance with clear statements in the New Testament (John 10:1–16; Luke 15:4–6). In this statue, which may have served as a tombstone, the artist succeeded, through strong emphasis on a concentric form, delineated by the lamb's back and legs and by the inner circles of the shepherd's hair and face, in focusing our attention on the latter's face. Time erased the paint from its eyes and some of the details, emphasizing an introspective quality in the shepherd's expression. The simple scene has thus obtained symbolic value: its representation has become an icon.

53

53. Garlanded Sarcophagus (early third century AD) Tel Barak, Caesarea district. Length 2.16 m. marble **(R)** This sarcophagus, richly adorned on all sides with representations of garlands and gods, in its centre a masque with gaping mouth, is thought to have been brought into the country from Asia Minor in antiquity.

54

54. Jewish Sarcophagus (first half of fourth century AD) Beth Shearim. Length 2.06 m. lead **(IM)** Lead sarcophagi were moulded in large sand or clay moulds, into which ornamentation had been stamped before pouring in the molten metal. They are fairly common in the Roman period, mainly in Syria-Palaestina, being widely used from the second to fourth centuries by the upper-middle classes, who could not afford marble or stone coffins, and felt above the use of mere wooden ones. While pagan coffins of the time still use Graeco-Roman mythological motifs, the comparatively late Christian coffins use the Cross only. The Jewish coffin from the famous catacombs of Beth Shearim (see also pls. 264–5) comes from a Sidonian workshop. To the basic motif of the vine-scroll with alternating jars and human heads, have been added the Jewish menorah, flanked by symbols for the High Holidays: ram's horn for the New Year, incense-shovel for the Day of Atonement and palm-branch with citrus fruit for the Feast of Tabernacles. (See also pl. 228.)

55

55. Amazons' Sarcophagus (early third century AD) Tel Barak, Caesarea district. Length 2.07 m. marble **(R)**
The front carries in high relief a beautiful representation of the fight between Greeks and Amazons. It was transported in antiquity from abroad, perhaps from Athens. The cover, in the shape of the deceased and his wife, reclining on a couch, remains unfinished, probably with the intention of having the work completed with portraits on the spot. This is not the only example in Israel where we find that this was never accomplished, perhaps because of the lack of suitable artists available locally.

56. *Colour plate III.* **Gold glass** (first half of fourth century AD) Rome. Diam. 0.09 m. glass and gold foil **(IM)**
Such glasses, carrying a picture cut in fine gold-foil between two sheets of glass, are in fact the bases of deep bowls, very few having survived undamaged. The representations are mostly of pagan or Christian character, though some twelve specimens with Jewish motifs have so far been recorded. Of these the Israel Museum has two, one being shown here. The upper register shows an open Torah-shrine, the scrolls of the Law exposed; the shrine is flanked by lions. The lower register shows two seven-branched menorahs, flanking the palm-branch, ram's horn, and citrus fruit—the usual attributes of the High Holidays. The Latin inscription above reads P I E Z E S E E L A R E S—a latinized Greek, to be interpreted as meaning 'drink—live merrily' or 'drink —thou shalt live!' in fact very much the meaning of the toast still used amongst Jews: *Lehaim!* (to Life!)

57. a–b–c. Lintels from the Basilica of the Holy Sepulchre (*c.* 1150–1180) Jerusalem. Length 3.75 m. marble

One of the two lintels, originally above the western entrance of the Crusaders' church of the Holy Sepulchre, was transferred in 1938 to the Rockefeller Museum when it was found to be threatened by total destruction by weathering and decay. The left-hand lintel (not shown here) recounts episodes connected with Jesus' life—the Last Supper (see detail to left)—in a rather conventional Romanesque style, while the right-hand lintel (above and to right) is executed in a free and fantastic style, probably by a European artist, influenced by early twelfth-century English illuminated manuscripts. One would suggest that the representation of legendary beasts

and birds of prey, flanked by seven
naked men caught in the coils of a spiral
foliage, some pointing to their sexual
organs (to right), has a symbolic meaning. For mediaeval Christianity, the
former represent malevolent and
dangerous demons: dragons personify
the Antichrist and heresy, if not the
Devil; sirens—female lust and tempta-
tion; the centaur—pride, arrogance,
male lust. The birds of prey may represent avarice. The men, their nakedness
then symbolizing lasciviousness, are
shown caught in a tree of deadly sins,
at the mercy of demons—a stark warning and a fitting antithesis to the orderly
representation of the life of Jesus, as
shown nearby.

58

58. Crown of a Domed Ceiling (724–743 AD) Khirbet al-Mafjar. Inner diam. 1.10 m. plaster **(R)**
The Umayyad palace in Khirbat al-Mafjar, near Jericho, was probably built, though never completed, by the Caliph Hisham ibn Abd al-Malik. The centre of the inner dome above one of the bathing rooms has an inner frame of grape-clusters, an astragal, and vine-leaves. There is a mixture of Sassanian, Graeco-Roman and local styles, also shown in the central representation of human heads which peer out from superimposed acanthus leaves with a central, six-petalled rosette. The human heads represent men and women, the former being indicated by a black-painted beard, the latter by earrings. Here it can be seen that the living form, which was later to disappear in Moslem architectural decoration, is already being absorbed by the rich and formalized plant-ornament, a forerunner of the arabesque.

59. Mary and Child (sixth century AD) Beth Shean. Height 0.13 m. terra cotta **(R)**
The ancient concept of the seated mother suckling her child was represented in the Eastern Mediterranean by the image of the Egyptian goddess Isis suckling Horus, as well as in Canaanite figurines. In this case, however, we have a very ancient Christian interpretation of the scene, existing at this early stage in the East alone, and there only in Coptic art. In wall-paintings, stone reliefs, and in writings of the early Coptic monks we find Jesus' Mother conceived in this manner, which was to become popular in the West only much later, in the Italian art of the fourteenth century, though appearing in rare cases in Romanesque art, the 'Virgin of Dom Rupert' of Liege being a good example. This modest figurine is an early forerunner and one which,

while humanizing Christ, does also in its strange, rather forbidding expression, keep the beholder at a distance.

60

60. Angel of St Matthew (second half of twelfth century) Belvoir. Height 1.15 m. stone **(R)**
The Crusader castle of Belvoir, also known as Coquet, overlooks the Jordan valley and the main roads running from south and west to east and north-east, across the fords between Beth Shean and Tiberias. Now known as Kokhav ha-Yarden, it was fortified about 1140 by Fulque d'Anjou, king of Jerusalem, and eventually garrisoned by the Order of the Knights Hospitallers. This high relief in French Romanesque style comes from the castle's upper-storey church. The angel, flying towards the left, holds a book in his hands, which are covered with a napkin, and thus seems to be the symbol of St Matthew, one of the four Evangelists surrounding the representation of the Christ in glory. The object above the angel is too damaged for identification, but it might have been a cloud. The sculpture shows signs of wilful destruction, the mouth of the angel being almost completely erased. This could have happened during the two Moslem demolitions—in 1219 and in 1227—perhaps with superstitious intent. This sculpture must have been made between the mid-twelfth century and January 1189, when the castle fell to Saladin. No sign of the existence of the symbols of the other three Evangelists has been found, nor the supposed central representation of Christ. Indeed, it is by no means certain that the church for which this relief was intended was ever finished.

61. *Colour plate VII.* **An Arab Woman's Jewellery** (late tenth century AD) Caesarea. Height 0.12 m. gold **(IM)**
This hoard was found inside the green-glazed jar hidden under a Crusader level of Caesarea; a Moslem woman must have hidden it away at the time of the Crusaders' siege in AD 1101. They display fine filigree and granulated work and the beautifully polished carnelian and glass-beads use the material to its best effect—all characteristic of the sophisticated city-culture of Fatimid Egypt.

62. The Carmel Aphrodite (fourth to third centuries BC). Present height 0.38 m. terracotta **(IM)**
This charming statuette was discovered in the surface layer of one of the Carmel caves, famous for its prehistoric finds. Aphrodite is here presented nude but for her necklace, anklet and a snake-shaped garter; she is leaning on an Ionic column. The style is classical and closely related to works of Praxiteles and his school. The garter is an exact representation of similar ornaments, often fashioned of precious metals, as worn by hetairai—Greek courtesans— in order to enhance their beauty. 62

63

64

63. Knight's Head (mid-thirteenth century) Montfort. Height 0.15 m. stone **(R)**
This stone-mason's work, a corbel, was found in one of the chambers added between 1230 and 1250 by a Teutonic Order to the fortress in western Galilee which they named Starkenberg. Founded in 1107 by French nobles, it was bought by the Order's Grand-Master, Hermann von Salza, in 1228; it fell to the Mamluk Sultan Baybars in 1271. This lively head, with eyes of lead inlay, has a strapped-on helmet in the shape of a truncated cone, formed originally by triangular pieces of metal attached to an iron circlet around the head. The nose-guard is lacking. Though this kind of helmet prevailed in the twelfth century, the place of its discovery suggests it was sculpted at a later date, perhaps representing a Knight of the Teutonic Order.

64. Lithographic Stone (thirteenth century) Montfort. Height 0.29 m. **(R)**
This stone seems to have been used to pattern softened leather or a similar material. The German eagle, presumably of the Teutonic Order which at the time held the castle, is set side by side with the fleur-de-lis, at that time already a French emblem, though not exclusively so.

65. *Colour plate IV.* **Egyptian Couple** (*c.* 1425 BC) Thebes. Height 0.35 m. wall painting **IM**
This painting comes from a tomb at Thebes in upper Egypt. It represents a woman and her husband holding a lotus flower, seated on a chair. It is a fine example of the sophisticated style of the end of the Eighteenth Dynasty, when Egyptian imperial might was at its zenith and the personal well-being of the capital's upper classes seemed assured.

66

67

66. Ceremonial Battle-Axe (beginning of sixteenth century) unknown provenance. Height 0.45 m. tinned iron **(R)**
Though such axes were used in battle, those as richly decorated as this one were kept for ceremonial occasions only, to be carried before the Sultan. The ornate Arabic inscription in its centre reads: 'Glory to our lord the Sultan King Qānsawh al Ashraf'. It thus seems to refer to one of the last Mamluks to rule Egypt and Syria, and to have belonged to Qānsawh al Ashraf al-Ghawri, who was defeated at Aleppo by the Turkish Sultan Sālim on 24 August 1516. This victory placed the country under Turkish rule for four hundred years.

(Illustrations 67–102 that follow in this chapter are all of items in the Israel Museum—IM.)

67. A Woman making a Sacrifice (seventh to early sixth century BC) Cyprus. Height 0.20 m. terracotta
The lower part of this figurine is made in the shape of a pillar, not unlike contemporary Judaean figurines (see pl. 187). The woman carries a dove as offering, her right hand raised in adoration. Around her neck she wears a large jewel and a heavy chain. She has a turban-like head-dress. Originally, this figurine was painted over and some of the paint, outlining her large eyes, can still be seen. Figurines of a similarly rustic but expressive character were discovered many years ago in a cave near Lapithos, Cyprus, and found their way to the British Museum in London.

68

69

68. Cofanetto (second half fifteenth century) Ferrara.
Height 0.08 m. silver, partly gilt, *niello*
Such caskets were often given to young ladies for their marriage, to hold keys and jewels. The one shown here belonged to a Jewish woman. Thus the front of the casket depicts the three main religious duties of Jewish women: baking bread for the Shabbat and symbolically sacrificing a small portion (*hallah*); dipping into the purifying ritual bath (*miqveh*); and kindling the Shabbat (and feastday) lights (*hadlaqat haner*). The duties are indicated in Hebrew inscriptions. The small dials on the lid have movable pointers, with Hebrew numerals and inscriptions in Hebrew letters to indicate the linen in the cupboard, some in Italian: *linziole* (sheets), *tovaglie* (towels or table-cloths), etc. Some are in Italian-Hebrew: *camicie mi ish* (men's shirts), and one in Hebrew only: *michnassaim* (trousers). The dials must have been used by the wife as a linen-list. The *cofanetto* is signed by the Jewish artisan who made it.

69. Kiddush Goblet (early seventeenth century) Germany.
Height 0.15 m. gold *repoussé*
The three scenes shown in medallions around the cup represent the sacrifice of Isaac, Jacob's dream and Jacob wrestling with the angel shown here. The dedicatory inscription, dated 1765, seems to be a later addition. Such goblets are used in Jewish domestic as well as synagogue rituals for the benediction over the wine, ushering in the Shabbat and Feast days or emphasizing joy at the marriage ceremony and at the circumcision of the new-born male child.

70. Hanukkah Candlestick (seventeenth century) Kielce, Poland. Height 1.46 m. brass

Such large candlesticks were made for synagogues as early as the twelfth century AD. The early ones are reported to have had lions for a base—clearly a Romanesque influence, since seven-branched candlesticks survive in Romanesque churches. The manufacture of eight-branched Hanukkah candlesticks, first for synagogues and also, albeit in a smaller size, for the home, circumvented the law against making a three-dimensional seven-branched menorah like the one in the Jerusalem Temple. It is significant that, in synagogues, it is put near the Holy Arch, usually to the right of it, in accordance with the position of the menorah in that temple. The large candlestick shown here comes from a Jewish community at Kielce, annihilated by the Nazis in World War II; it was given to the museum in their memory.

71. *Colour plate XLII.* **The Bird's Head Haggadah** (end fourteenth century) Germany. Forty-seven leaves of 0.27 × 0.185 m. vellum

The Haggadah is a traditional collection of benedictions, stories, commentaries and songs, to be read by the head of the family to his household on Passover-eve. Most of the text stems from the first centuries AD; the earliest surviving manuscript goes back to the tenth century; this is one of the earliest surving illuminated Haggadahs. Its peculiarity is in the rendering of all human heads as those of birds, in an ultra-orthodox wish to refrain from presenting the human form. It is also interesting that all the Jews shown in these drawings wear the special Jew's hat, forced on them by their Christian overlords in order to make them distinguishable from the Gentiles.

70

73

74

72. Sennacherib Prism (691 BC) Assyria. Height 0.71 m. pottery

This prism describes, in cuneiform characters and in the Akkadian language, the Babylonian king's campaign and victories in Philistia and Judah, where he overcame king Hezekiah in 701 BC, besieging Jerusalem and taxing the country heavily. This historically important text, paralleling the Biblical accounts in 2 Kings, 18–19, Isaiah 36–37, and 2 Chron. 32:21, was distributed by Sennacherib throughout his realm in large numbers. Today only two more complete copies have survived, one in the British Museum, London, and one in the Oriental Institute, Chicago.

73. Nahmanides Seal (thirteenth century) Acre. Diam. 0.022 m. cast copper

This seal was found in 1972 near Tell Kisan, in the Acre plain. It has a pierced handle, and could thus be worn suspended round the neck. The Hebrew inscription reads: 'Moses son of Rabbi Nahman of restful soul (*i.e.* the late) of Gerona—have vigour!' It is thus the personal seal of Nahmanides (1194–1270), Spanish-Jewish rabbi, philosopher, poet and physician, who was born in Gerona, Catalonia. In 1267 he travelled to Acre, then, in 1268, to Jerusalem where he re-dedicated the first Jewish synagogue after the defeat of the Crusader Latin Kingdom. He then returned to Acre where he died. It seems likely that he lost the seal, of simple design and script, probably made by himself, on the way from Acre to Jerusalem, via Megiddo. (For the seal's face, see p. 13.)

74. Relief Amphora (seventh century BC) Crete. Height 1.27 m. pottery

These large storage amphoras were decorated with applied reliefs in the so-called Daedalic style, essentially of an orientalizing character expressed in its heraldic formalism. Very few complete specimens have survived; most, as this one, have had to be reconstructed from fragments. The upper register shows a winged goddess, completely frontal, flanked by antithetic sphinxes. The metopes in the band below show the recurring motif of a rider, urging on his horse. Having seen Western influences in some local antiquities (i.e. pls. 34, 39, 40), it is interesting to note here one of the many instances of East influencing West.

75

75

75. Hanukkah Lamp (1574) Holland. Height 0.23 m. bronze

The eight lights of the lamp are lit on the eight eves of the mid-winter festival of Hanukkah, celebrating the victory in 165 BC of the Maccabees over the Seleucids, the liberation of Jerusalem and the re-dedication of its Temple. The lighting ceremony is performed at home as well as in the synagogue, each night one additional light being kindled. A ninth lamp, the 'servant' (*Shamash*), is used for the kindling of the feast-lights, to ensure that secular use will be made of the 'servant' only and not of the hallowed lights. The oldest surviving Hanukkah lamps date from the fourteenth century, except for a single specimen in marble, from southern France, which may be of the twelfth century. The usual type has the eight lamps in a row holding oil and a wick, backed by an ornamental wall, often in openwork. This rather simple and restrained specimen uses the Hebrew formula pronounced when kindling the lights, which recounts the reasons for the feast and declares the holiness of these lights. This modest late-Gothic creation, with its rather Nordic horses—or 'dragons'—heads, has the signature of its maker, Meir Heilprin, at the end of the inscription.

76. Synagogue Doors and Lintel (twelfth and thirteenth century, respectively) Fostat, Egypt. Height 2.40 and 0.20 m. wood

The pitch-pine panels are carved in a purely Fatimid style, prevalent at that period in Egypt and Syria, characterized by arabesque scrolls, combined with birds, animals and figures, all done in high relief. Nothing in the representation points to any specially Jewish characteristics though the doors come from the ancient Ben-Ezra synagogue of Fostat, Egypt. The Hebrew inscription above, which refers to a Rabbi Solomon who died in his youth, comes from the same synagogue. Tradition has it that Rabbi Maimonides (1135–1204), the great Spanish-Jewish sage, philosopher and physician, prayed there.

76

76

77. The Vittorio Veneto Synagogue
(1701) Vittorio Veneto, north of Venice.
Floor space 7 × 13 m. height 7 m.
gilt wood, brass, silver
This synagogue had already fallen into
disuse some fifty years ago; the local
authorities therefore agreed in 1964 to
its transfer to Jerusalem, where it was
reconstructed in exact detail. The
interior arrangement is in accordance
with Spanish-Jewish (Sephardic) ritual,
men sitting along the walls and women
in the latticed gallery above. The
cantor (*shaliah zibbur*—lit. 'messenger
of the congregation') stands on a dais
near the doors, facing both the congregation and the Holy Arch, always
oriented towards Jerusalem. This syna-

gogue's style mixes baroque and neo-
classical elements. The comparative
simplicity of the interior contrasts with
the richly adorned shrine holding the
Torah. This emphasis upon the supremacy of the Divine Law has remained
throughout the ages the prime characteristic of the faith, in both ceremonial
and daily practice.

78. *Colour plate VI.* **Hallah Cover** (nineteenth century) Jerusalem. Length 1.30
m. embroidery on linen
Such covers are used on the traditional
Shabbat-eve table to cover the specially
prepared braided wheat-loaves (*Hallah*).
For its use, see the ethnographic exhibit

(pl. 198). The embroidery shown here
was executed by a Jewish housewife
in Jerusalem after a drawing by Jacob
Janover (1840–1910), a local craftsman,
who also did the wall-paintings of the
Hurvah synagogue in the Jewish
quarter of Jerusalem (destroyed by the
Arabs in 1948). The cover shows a
naively drawn itinerary of the Holy
Places. A hymn greeting the Angels of
Peace, who enter the Jewish home on
Shabbat eve, frames the sacred places—
the tombs of the Fathers and Kings of
the nation. The inner frame contains a
benediction for the members of the
household and shows a representation
of the Western Wall, with the mosques
of Temple Hill in the background.

79

79. *Colour plate V (of detail).* **The Horb Synagogue** (1735) Horb am Main, Germany. Floor space 8 × 5 m. wood
Few wooden Jewish places of worship survive, those which still existed in this century having nearly all been destroyed by the Nazis. The one shown here was kept in the Bamberg Museum, the authorities having agreed to its exhibition in Jerusalem. Such painted synagogues were fairly common in Poland, and the painter of the Horb synagogue identifies himself in his signature as having come from Brody. The barrel-ceiling is richly painted with baroque floral ornamentation carrying a fantastic variety of animals and birds. The upper-west side shows the representation of two heraldic lions, blowing trumpets, flanking a medallion which bears a sentence from the High Holidays' liturgy. Above them are shown two *shofars* (ram's horns) used at the New Year. The representation is flanked by a picture of fruits and palm-branches to the right, symbolizing the Feast of Tabernacles (*Sukkoth*), and to its left by a picture of Jerusalem. The east side carries a canopy, its tip held by heraldic lions, over the Torah-shrine. At its sides are flower-ornaments, above it medallions with Biblical and liturgical texts, as well as the artist's signature and the date of his work.

80. Torah Crown (1793) Germany. Height 0.20 m. silver

The crowning of the Scroll of the Law, containing the five books of Moses (the *Torah*), is known to have existed as a Jewish custom since the Middle Ages, though the oldest surviving specimens cannot be dated before the seventeenth century. The concept of conferring royal distinction only upon the Divine Law is Jewish; its style however is dictated by the period and country of execution. This specimen shows in openwork the representation of a pair of hands, fingers spread in the ceremonial gesture used since the Second Temple time by descendants of priestly families (*Cohens*) at the end of the Feast-day liturgy in the synagogue, when solemnly pronouncing over the congregation the triple benediction prescribed in Numbers 6:22–27. Popular belief has it that the unseen presence of the Lord (the *Shekhina*), hovers at benediction over the priest's hands, which are therefore covered by the prayer-shawl (*tallit*).

80

81. Bukharian Jews' Robes (late nineteenth century)

To the right, a man's wedding coat, embroidered in gold, silver and silk threads; to the left, a married woman's ceremonial dress, fashioned in material woven in Russia. These Jewish dresses, some of great splendour, combine motifs of Central Asia, Persia and Turkey.

83

82. *Colour plate VIII.* **Yemenite Bride** (recent) San'a, Yemen. Brocade, silver and gilt beads, pearls, coral
This elaborate dress—the *tishbuq lulu*—was used at the main marriage ceremony, a celebration taking some two weeks, in which both bride and groom wore different dresses in accordance with each ceremony. The jewellery is characteristic of Jewish Yemenite silversmith's work, a trade which was almost exclusively in Jewish hands in the Yemen, since transferred to Israel by this community.

83. **Emanuel de Witte** (1618–1692, Holland) *Portuguese Synagogue in Amsterdam* (c. 1680) 1.08 × 1.23 m. oil on canvas
This picture, executed when the Delft painter was doing some of his best work, shows the famous synagogue which still stands in Amsterdam, as it was when built in 1675, and the chancel from where the service is conducted at the rear, according to Spanish-Jewish rites (see pl. 77). It demonstrates de Witte's two major contributions to paintings of church interiors: he expresses the mood in contrasting light and shadow and also transfers this contrast into the psychological sphere by introducing gaily dressed visitors, accompanied by elegant dogs in the foreground, while in the background sombre worshippers attend to divine service.

84. *Colour plate IX.* **Jacob Gerritz** (1594–1651) and **Albert Cuyp** (1620–1691, Holland). *Return from the Hunt* (1641). 1.55 × 2.45 m. oil on canvas.
Of this family of Dordrecht painters, Albert was to become the best known. At the time this picture was painted, he was still a young man and thus only entrusted with painting the background: the cows, the farmstead, the far-away church steeple and the wide, somewhat cloudy sky. The figures in the foreground were most probably the work of his father, Jacob Gerritz.

85

86

85. Rembrandt Harmensz van Rijn
(1606–1669, Holland) *The Healing of
Tobit* (c. 1642–44). 0.098 × 0.0138 m.
pen, bistre and wash on paper
It is the good fortune of the Israel
Museum to possess this fine sketch by
Rembrandt, who had a very special
feeling both for Holy Writ and for the
Jews, in whose neighbourhood he lived
from 1639, at Jooden-Breestraat; this
was near the place where, some years
after his death, the great Portuguese
synagogue was to be built (see pl. 83).
The sketch illustrates one of the episodes
from the book of Tobit (3:17): Tobias
healing the blindness of his father, Tobit.

86. Jean-Honoré Fragonard (1732–
1806, France) *The Artist's Father.* 0.25 ×
0.28 m. brownish-red chalk on paper.
This marvellous portrait of an old man
nursing his gouty leg evokes the warm-
ness of the artist's place of birth—
Grasse, in Provence. Here he has left the
seductive ladies and formal landscapes
of his large paintings for one of his inti-
mate drawings. We are privileged to get
a glimpse into 'the diary of his imagination' as the brothers de Goncourt described this part of his work.

87

88

87. Fernand Léger (1881–1955, France) *Composition with Person* (1924). 0.50 × 0.65 m. oil on canvas
Léger's pictures always expressed his robust personality, his predilection for simple people and their strength. Here volumes are related through action and counter-action, be they machine, house or man. (see also pl. XXIV/154).

88. Jules Pascin (1885–1930, Spain) *Portrait of William Howard* (1909). 0.55 × 0.46 m. oil on cardboard
A Spanish-Jewish painter, born in Bulgaria, and belonging to the Ecole de Paris, Pascin's sharp and often biting wit was normally aimed at his female models. Indeed, one is included in this portrait of the German painter, Howard. The Israel Museum has over a hundred items in its Pascin collection.

89

89. Maurice Utrillo (1883–1955,
France) *The Asylum at Montmélian* (*c.*
1910). 0.73 × 0.92 m. oil on canvas
A broken-down alcoholic at the age of
eighteen, Utrillo took up painting
following medical advice, though he
lapsed from time to time. In most of his
pictures, he gave us a loving and very
Parisian view of his city (see pl. 132)
and the neighbouring villages. This
picture, however, done at the end of his
'white period', shows the asylum, which
lies north of Grenoble.

90. *Colour plate X.* **Paul Cézanne**
(1839–1906, France) *Country House by the
Riverside* (1888–90). Oil on canvas.
Cézanne here achieves his aim, to
'create constructions after nature'. Visiting the museum, one never fails to be
delighted by the perfect balance of form
and colour in this picture.

91. Joseph Zaritsky (born 1891, Russia) *Safed* (*c.* 1924). 0.63 × 0.61 m. watercolour on black underlining

Having studied art in Kiev, Zaritsky settled in Jerusalem in 1922, living in Tel Aviv from 1927. In 1948, he was one of the founders of the 'New Horizons' group, in which he became for many years the moving force of Israeli abstract art (see also pl. XXXIV/175).

91

92. *Colour plate XII.* **Georges Braque** (1882–1963, France) *Trees at La Ciotat* (1907). 0.362 × 0.465 m. Oil on canvas. Braque's bold handling of colour and form makes this one of the pictures which resulted in his inclusion for a time in the Fauvist group.

93. *Colour plate XIII.* **Egon Schiele** (1890–1918, Austria) *The City* (1915). 1.10 × 1.40 m. oil on canvas. The major part of this young Expressionist's work was dedicated to the drawing of the human form, with a strong emphasis on the erotic. Only a fraction of his paintings show city scenes. Both themes are developed in a sombre mood, as though foreshadowing death, which overtook him at an early age.

94. *Colour plate XVII.* **Pablo Picasso** (1881–1973, Spain) *Seated Woman* (1949). 1 × 0.81 m. oil on canvas. One of the four oil-paintings by Picasso owned by the Israel Museum. The museum is also fortunate in possessing about a fifth of Picasso's graphic work (for his sculpture, see pl. 103).

95. *Colour plate XIV.* **Reuben Rubin** (born 1893, Romania) *Seascape from a Hill* (1927). 0.65 × 0.81 m. oil on canvas. Rubin was to return from Israel to his country of birth twice: as a young artist of rising fame during the First World War, and as Israel's Ambassador in 1948–50. This picture of Tiberias is a good example of his almost childlike joy in the earth, water, and sky of the Land of the Bible. (See also pl. 153.)

96. *Colour plate XXVI.* **Mordechai Ardon** (born 1896, Poland) *Towards Jerusalem* (1962). 1.30 × 1.62 m. oil on canvas. Ardon's craftsmanship and fundamental respect towards his material, acquired at the Bauhaus, and the reflected lyricism of his teachers— among them Kandinsky and Klee—is combined with his own mystical viewpoint, the product of his Hassidic childhood home. He is considered one of Israel's outstanding painters. This is one of a number of large paintings which Ardon devoted to Jerusalem, where he has lived and worked since 1933.

97. *Colour plate XXVIII.* **Arie Aroch** (born 1908, Russia) *The High Commissioner* (1965). 1.16 × 0.75 m. oil on wood. The artist, who came to this country in 1924, served Israel as Ambassador to Brazil and Sweden from 1956 to 1962. (See also pl. 159.)

84

98. The Billy Rose Art Garden (1965)
Israel Museum, Jerusalem
This garden, seen here from the north-east, was planned by Isamu Noguchi, the great American architect of Japanese origin. With terraces and walls built of locally quarried stone, Noguchi succeeded in creating spaces well attuned both to the surrounding ancient hills and to the modern sculpture within. He added his own sculpture, an altar-like fountain, set upon the terrace (background left) where the water trickles down between the huge stones. It is a reminder of Noguchi's rock-and-water garden at Unesco's headquarters in Paris and a distant echo of the Japanese concepts of such gardens.

99. a–b. Victor Vasarely (born 1908, Hungary) *Screen* (1967). 2.50 × 4.33 m. steel
A Parisian since 1930, the artist created this screen especially for the Israel Museum—in his own definition: 'a deep-kinetic positive-negative work of steel strips'. The two photos try to catch some of the pleasure gained by a visitor to the Sculpture Garden, where this work achieves the artist's aim of 'architectonic integration'.

100. Auguste Rodin (1841–1917, France) *Study for Balzac* (1892). Height 1.28 m. bronze
This study for the Balzac monument is one of the many which Rodin did in the early nineties of the last century. Originally made in plaster or terracotta, no more than twelve were cast of each study, mostly after Rodin's death. For the Balzac monument, Rodin began, as was his habit, by reading the works of his subject, visiting his birthplace, and studying all the possible evidence. Thus the head and the folded arms conform to a portrait of the writer, done in 1837 by Louis Boulenger. The final version, however, had the hands lowered to close the folds of Balzac's famous dressing-gown, hung over his shoulders like a cowl, his head flung back. This latter work was exhibited in 1898 at the Paris Salon and rejected by the Writers' Society. It took Paris another forty-one years to have the statue cast in bronze and erected on the Boulevard Mont-parnasse. (See also pl. 123.)

101

101. David Smith (1906–65, USA)
Cubi VI (1963). Height 2.85 m. stainless
steel
One of the twenty-eight variations of
this American artist's creations which
he named 'cubi', and worked in stainless
steel, though most of his statues are of
iron. The work is set up in the garden
as the artist conceived it: '. . . in a
particular sense I have used atmosphere
in a reflective way on the surfaces. They
are coloured by the sky and the surroundings, the green or blue of water.
Some are down by the water and some
are by the mountains. They reflect the
colours. They are designed for out-
doors.' (*David Smith by David Smith*,
New York, 1968, p. 123.)

XI. **Paul Signac,** *St Cloud.* Tel Aviv Museum. (Note 131)

XII. **Georges Braque,** *Trees at La Ciotat,* 1907. The Israel Museum, Jerusalem. (Note 92)

XIII. **Egon Schiele,** *The City*, 1915. The Israel Museum, Jerusalem. (Note 93)

XIV. **Reuben Rubin,** *Seascape from a Hill*, 1927. The Israel Museum, Jerusalem. (Note 95)

XV. **James Ensor,** *Ma Chambre préférée*, 1892. Tel Aviv Museum. (Note 130)

XVI. **Chaim Soutine,** *Landscape at Cagnes*. Tel Aviv Museum. (Note 143)

XVII. **Pablo Picasso,** *Seated Woman,* 1949. The Israel Museum, Jerusalem. (Note 94)

XVIII. **Kees van Dongen,** *Cabaret.* Tel Aviv Museum. (Note 138)

XIX. **Edouard Vuillard,** *The Model at Rest*, 1910. Tel Aviv Museum. (Note 134)

XX. **Pierre Auguste Renoir,** *Nude*. Tel Aviv Museum. (Note 135)

XXI. **Marc Chagall,** *Jew with Torah*. Tel Aviv Museum. (Note 144)

102

103

102. Menashe Kadishman (born 1932, Israel) *Suspense* (1966). Height 3.02 m. painted steel
Israeli born and locally trained, this sculptor divides his time between Israel and England. In his work he achieves what at first appears to be an impossible balance.

103. Pablo Picasso (1881–1973, Spain) *Profile* (1967). Height 5.33 m. concrete-cast, sandblasted.
This beautiful cast was prepared by a team from Norway on the eve of the Six Day War. They accomplished this in spite of a delay of some weeks, leaving Jerusalem enriched by this majestic silhouette. (See also pl. XVII/94.)

104. Ossip Zadkine (1890–1967, France) *Heroic Orpheus* (1954). Height 2.18 m. bronze

This work was created in 1954 by the great French artist, of Russian-Jewish origin. Here Orpheus, his lyre, and Eluard's poem, which covers the whole figure, are combined to great effect. Paul Eluard's 'Song to Freedom' was written in 1942 during France's occupation, and the mass-deportation of her Jews:

> *Sur toute chair accordée*
> *Sur le front de mes amis*
> *Sur chaque main qui se tend*
> *j'écris ton nom*
> *Liberté*

(See also pl. 142.)

105. Jacques Lipchitz (1891–1973, France) *Ploumanach* (1926). Height 0.21 m. bronze

Ploumanach, a summer resort in Brittany, provided the artist with the image of rocks on the coast, undercut by the waves and held in suspension. The concept achieved its final form in 1930, in the bronze statue now at the Museum of Modern Art, New York. This is one of some one hundred and thirty bronze casts of the artist's sketches, presented by his brother to the Israel Museum. Their permanent exhibition in one of its pavilions provides the visitor with a unique opportunity to study this sculptor's work. (See also pl. 129.)

107

106. Alexander Calder (born 1898, USA) *Mobile-Stabile* (1966). Height 2.80 m. painted steel
Coloured shapes move endlessly upon a black base which has been set on a roof of the Museum, overlooking the Valley of the Cross. Changing slowly or swiftly as it moves in the wind, it gives pleasure both to museum visitors, who can see this pleasant sculpture through some of the gallery's large windows, and to the strollers in the valley below.

107. Henry Moore (born 1898, England) *Vertebrae* (1968). Length 7.10 m. bronze
Of the impressive series of reclining figures which Moore has done throughout his life, this is one of the latest: pared down to its skeleton, mighty, antediluvian, it yet gazes confidently into the future. (For other work by this artist see pls. 124 and 145.)

108. *Colour plate XXXII.* **Niki de St Phalle** (born 1930, France) *Golem* (1972). Height 8 m. painted steel-reinforced concrete.
This friendly monster was erected in one of the western suburbs of Jerusalem under the auspices of the Israel Museum. A huge toy, its three slides in constant use by the children of the neighbourhood, it includes some of the ideas expressed by this artist in her huge *She*, which was put up in 1966 at the Museum of Modern Art, Stockholm. Tinguely co-operated in the construction of this *Golem* as he had done with *She* and other works by Niki de St Phalle.

109

109. Youth Wing Activities Israel Museum, Jerusalem.
To absorb the past, to play in the present, and learn to build
the future—one hopes this is the aim of the youth wing of
any good museum. At the Museum it is done with guided
tours, special exhibitions and lectures, courses and creative
activities of all kinds—one of which is shown in this brief but
happy moment.

110. Jean Tinguely (born 1925, Switzerland) *xk³* (1965).
Height 4 m. iron
Creakily rotating and bobbing since it was set up by Tinguely
just before the opening of the Israel Museum, this movement-
machine has done its creator's bidding: 'condemned like
Sisyphus to repeat all the time the same action'.

OTHER JERUSALEM MUSEUMS

The three major religions of the country have their museums in Jerusalem, the oldest having the newest museum. Housed since 1958 in the Chief Rabbinate's building, the **Isaac Wolfson Museum** displays all aspects of Jewish religious life, from antiquity to the present, including material from all parts of the Diaspora. The collection includes an important group of Hebrew manuscripts and rare prints.

Collections of the Catholic Orders, having been early in the field of local museums, concentrated less on the religious than on the general archaeological aspects. Most of these are not open to the public. The most important, however, the **Convent of the Flagellation** on the Via Dolorosa in Old Jerusalem, kept since 1931 by Franciscan Fathers, opens its fine museum to visitors upon request. Besides many important finds from their own excavations and an extensive collection of coins, the Fathers keep in this museum a rich collection pertaining to the history of local Christianity in general and their own Order in particular.

The Greek Orthodox Church and the Armenian Patriarchates both have very fine collections of ecclesiastical vestments and vessels,

111. The Jerusalem City Museum
Part of this museum is housed in the oldest surviving building of the city: Phasael, one of the three towers which King Herod built about 30 BC for his palace, naming it after his elder brother. When the victorious Romans destroyed Jerusalem in AD 70 they spared these towers 'in order to demonstrate to posterity what kind of city it was, and how well fortified, which the Roman valour subdued', as Josephus has it (*War of the Jews*, VII:1). While the two other towers disappeared in later developments and wars in this city, Phasael was incorporated into later fortifications of the city's citadel, called by the people the 'Tower of David'. Today the citadel includes buildings of the Umayyads, the Crusaders, the Mamluks and the Turks; it also houses the city's museum of history and ethnography.

112. The Palombo Museum (1967)
Jerusalem
This museum on Mount Zion, formerly
David Palombo's studio, now displays
much of his assembled work. Born in
1920, he died in a road accident aged
forty-six. In a few short years he created
the gates of the Knesset (Parliament)
and those of the Yad Vashem Memorial
Hall, in addition to other monumental
works: welding iron into perfect expressions of a people's ancient sorrows
and young hopes. Much of his explosive
personality, his gentle strength and his
deep love and understanding of the
language of wood, stone and iron, can
be seen and felt in this small museum
outside Zion Gate.

as well as rare illuminated manuscripts. Both have plans to open their own museums to the general public.

On the Temple Mount—*Haram al-Sherif* (lit. 'the Noble Sanctuary')—stands the Dome of the Rock, built over the Rock in AD 691 by the Umayyad Caliph Abd el-Malik, which was first used as a Canaanite 'high place' and twice carried the Holy of Holies of the Temple of the Lord. The **Islamic Museum** was inaugurated on the Mount in 1923 by the Moslem Wakf (religious endowment fund) and is housed in the additions built by the Crusaders to the Al-Aqsa congregational mosque nearby. It contains important architectural details from the Dome of the Rock and the Al-Aqsa mosque, removed during repairs to the latter, which was damaged several times by earthquakes. These details are mainly wooden soffits and beams, Umayyad work of high quality, but there is also a quantity of stucco and stone work; the iron fence put around the Rock by the Crusaders; and the ancient capitals from the Al-Aqsa mosque. All this has from time to time been replaced by excellent modern copies—especially at the Al-Aqsa, and thus survives in this museum. Ancient Korans and manuscripts complete the collection.

The Jerusalem City Museum: though housing the National Museum and other fine smaller ones, Israel's capital has only now begun to look after its own needs. It has secured for the purpose a highly appropriate building complex, Jerusalem's Citadel, the foundations of which belong to the Hasmonean period. The site was opened by the President in 1973 with a special exhibition of the finds

113. Synagogue Lamps (1719) Cochin, India. Height 0.49 and 0.47 m. bronze   (Wolfson Museum) These lamps lighted the synagogue of the ancient Jewish community of Cochin, many of whose members are now living in Israel. The lamps were cast in the lost wax process, including their dated Hebrew dedicatory inscriptions.

114. Spice-Box (eighteenth century) probably Vienna. Height 0.30 m. silver-filigree; semi-precious stones and painted *émaillé* insets

(Wolfson Museum)

The use of burned incense was discontinued in Jewish ceremony after the destruction of the Second Temple in AD 70, though still customary as an agreeable ending for banquets, in accordance with Roman custom (see pl. 231). The use of the strong-smelling spices had, however, become a Jewish custom from the first century AD onwards, as part of the short religious ceremony, marking the end of the Shabbat, the *Havdalah* (lit.: 'Separation'). To symbolize the separation between Shabbat and week-days a lighted candle is extinguished with some of the wine used for the benediction. Jewish lore conceived of an additional, festive soul, which is bestowed upon the believer during Shabbat. As this soul would leave him at the end of the holy day, his spirit should be strengthened with strong-smelling herbs and spices. Though this custom also goes back to the first century AD, spice-boxes used at the ceremony survive only from the sixteenth century onwards. Many have fantastic forms: flowers, birds, even an occasional railway-engine. The majority of the spice-boxes made in Europe, however, are in the form of a tower. The very rare spice-box shown here is one of three of its kind known to have survived; the other two are at the Musée Cluny, Paris, and the Jewish Museum, New York. The small *émaillé* insets show scenes from the Bible, while the Hebrew inscription on the medallions at the foot of the little tower contain part of the text used at the ceremony: 'The Jews had light and gladness, joy and honour' (Esther 8:16).

114

from the Temple Hill excavations. In towers that still stand after two thousand years of strife, the visitor will be able to see examples of the history and ethnography of the city's many peoples and the three major religions, all to be set in a permanent exhibition, now in active planning.

The Old Jewish Court recently opened its gates in the Old City. It reconstructs the life and customs of the local Jewish community in the last century.

The Palombo Museum stands outside Zion Gate. It shows the work of a young Israeli artist who was killed accidentally: David Palombo (1920–1966). This museum too is subsidized by the city.

115

115. The Dome of the Rock (end of seventh century AD) Height 35.30 m. (excluding the crescent)

Behind the rows of Moslem worshippers, performing one of the five daily prayers prescribed by the Koran, rises the Dome of the Rock, sometimes erroneously called the Mosque of Omar. It was built by the Umayyad Caliph, Abd el-Malik, to outshine the Anastasis, Church of the Resurrection (nowadays Basilica of the Holy Sepulchre) and in order to rival Mecca as a place of pilgrimage. The magnificent dome of the building, which takes its octagonal plan from that of the aforementioned Anastasis, covers the Rock, which carried the Holy of Holies of two Jewish Temples: the one built by King Solomon and destroyed by Nebuchadnezzar (*c.* 960 to 586 BC), and that built by King Herod and destroyed by Titus (*c.* 20 BC to AD 70).

Perfectly conceived in its fundamental geometry, an octagon holding the drum upon which the cupola rises, this building stands, the original mosaics still intact, as it was erected at the end of the seventh century. Its dome fell only once, in the earthquake of 1016, and was quickly repaired. Firm upon the Rock, yet a light construction based on arches, wooden beams and dome, the building has withstood all subsequent quakes which damaged or destroyed the Aqsa mosque nearby, built upon Herodian and later structures with heavy walls, columns and roof. Only few replacements of damaged parts proved necessary to the Dome of the Rock, which in later ages was decorated externally with beautiful Turkish tiles. These were renewed from time to time by local Armenian potters, specially brought to Jerusalem in the early nineteen-twenties for the purpose, and still practising their craft in the city.

Islam has identified this place as the spot of Mohammed's ascent to heaven, before returning to Mecca, in his miraculous night flight as recounted in the Koran 17:1: 'Praise be to Him, who has brought His servant, to show him some miracles, in a night's journey from the Holy Temple [i.e. the *Kaaba* of Mecca] to the Furthermost Temple [in Arabic: *el Mesjid el Aqsa*]'.

116. *Colour plate XLIII.* **Illuminated Initial** (end of fourteenth century AD) Italy. 247 leaves parchment: height 0.56 × 0.46 m.   (Convent of the Flagellation)

This adorns a page of an Antiphonary of the Saints which contains a song for the day of St. John the Baptist. According to the dedication it was given by John of Gaunt, son of Edward III and father of Henry IV of England, to 'the Brethren of the Holy Mount Sion'. It was probably brought by the latter king to the Holy Land in 1392. The miniaturist has used the upright of the Capital M to separate the scene of Salome's dance before her stepfather, Herod Antipas, and the decapitation of the Baptist, whose head is brought to her on a platter.

117. *Colour plate XLI.* **Koran** (ninth century AD). Each leaf 0.23 × 0.30 m. parchment   (Islamic Museum)

The Koran (lit. 'Readings') contains the revelations, which, by tradition Mohammed received from the Angel Gabriel as messages from the Lord. A revised and authorized version was prepared in AD 651, containing 114 *suras* (i.e. chapters) of greatly differing lengths. Many beautifully written Korans exist, the earliest surviving being that of AD 784–5, in the Cairo Library. The earliest copy in Jerusalem is the one shown here. It contains the second half of the Koran, beginning with *sura* 19. Though a note on the lower margin ascribes the penmanship to Mohammed ibn al-Hassan, one of the two sons of Fatima, the Prophet's daughter, and thus to the eighth century, it is in fact a very fine manuscript of the ninth century. The stately ancient Arabic script used here, the *Cufic*, was in the eleventh century slowly replaced by the cursive *Naskhi*, which is still in common use. Inscribed on the leaves shown here are the last two short *suras*, containing incantations against evil magic.

118. *Colour plate XLIV.* **Holy Ark Doors.** (seventeenth century) Cracow. Height 1.30 m. painted wood

                    (Wolfson Museum)

These doors came from an old synagogue in Cracow formerly one of the major centres of Jewish life in Poland. They are carved and painted to represent the dictum of Rabbi Judah, a sage of the second century AD: 'Be strong as the leopard and swift as the eagle, fleet as the deer and bold as the lion (to do the will of your Father in Heaven).' The unbracketed words are carved in Hebrew under the crown. The symbolic animals are shown with the Tree of Life, symbol of the Torah, the Divine Law. Some peculiarities in the rendering of this theme, as, for instance, the eagle feeding its young, are thought to reflect Cabbalistic tendencies current in this community at the time. One may also observe realistic details, as for instance the actual buildings of Cracow, shown on the upper left.

119

119. Carved Soffit (eighth century AD)
Al-Aqsa Mosque, Jerusalem. Height
0.95 m. wood   (Islamic Museum)
One of the soffits which held the
wooden beams between the arches of the
Aqsa Mosque, standing at the south
end of Jerusalem's Temple Hill, called
in Arabic *Haram esh-Sherif* ('The Noble
Sanctuary'). This mosque stands near
the spot where Islam's first Caliph,
Omar, built a small mosque in AD 640,
and Abd el-Malik his larger mosque
about AD 710. This and subsequent
buildings were destroyed by earthquakes, to which this mosque proved
much more vulnerable than the archi-
tecturally and topographically sounder
Dome of the Rock nearby. A structural
survey in the early nineteen-thirties
proved the necessity of a thorough reconstruction, at which time the beams
and soffits and other architectural
details were removed for safekeeping,
most to the adjacent museum. The
carving still shows traits of the Byzantine style and was probably the work of
local Christians, as proven by a Greek
inscription, inked by one of the workers
on a beam. They should thus be considered of original eighth-century work,
being re-used after each earthquake.

110

120

120. Passover-Cup (seventeenth century) Germany. Height 0.09 m. ivory

(Wolfson Museum)

This German Baroque cup bears in miniature-relief two biblical stories, one of which is only indirectly connected with the feast: Moses and Aaron before Pharaoh (Ex. 7) and, as shown here, Joseph fleeing from Potiphar's wife (Gen. 39:12). The cup is, astonishingly enough, the work of a Jew, who signed it at the base in Hebrew: 'Handiwork of Joseph, son of Rabbi Isaac.' It was perhaps the artist's name that suggested this theme to him, rather rare in Jewish iconography and certainly unique in its frank rendering on a vessel, clearly marked by the Hebrew inscription on its rim 'Let My People Go' as intended for the solemn Passover-Eve service, celebrated in the Jewish home.

121

121. Detail of a Frieze (end of seventh century AD) Dome of the Rock, Jerusalem. Height 0.50 m. gilded marble
(Islamic Museum)
These flat reliefs, showing small arches which frame stylized plants, come from one of the capitals of the eight heavy piers which carry the dome's inner octagon. They date from AD 691. Damaged by an earthquake, they were replaced by copies.

122

122. Convent of the Flagellation

The Franciscan Order built here a small chapel in Jerusalem in 1838. The present building includes a museum and dates from 1927. It marks the beginning of the Via Dolorosa, the traditional Way of the Cross, seen here with the so-called Ecce-Homo Arch in the background. The convent's name refers to the scourging of Jesus; the name of the arch to the words of the Roman Governor when exposing Jesus to the crowd (John 19:1–5). The existing arch dates from the second century AD.

THE MUSEUMS
OF TEL AVIV
THE TEL AVIV MUSEUM

The city museums of Israel, often originating from private collections founded by private initiative, were usually taken over by the various municipalities. In 1906 a group of Jews founded, on the dunes north of Jaffa, a suburb which was to become the modern and thriving city of Tel Aviv. One of the founders of this city and its first mayor, Meir Dizengoff, donated his own house to the city in 1931. Here was established a museum of art, the **Tel Aviv Museum**. Here too, in the main exhibition hall, the independence of the State of Israel was declared in 1948.

In 1958 this museum, having acquired an important collection of pictures and statues, including valuable works by James Ensor, Vlaminck, Utrillo, and Chagall, built new premises—the **Helena Rubenstein Pavilion**, which, since 1971, has been used for temporary exhibitions. The present **Tel Aviv Museum**, planned by I. Yashar and D. Eitan, was opened in 1971. Its major collections are housed in four main galleries. These include a small but select group of European paintings of the sixteenth and seventeenth centuries, and a fine group of paintings and sculptures of the late nineteenth and twentieth centuries, including the above-mentioned groups of pictures and works by Archipenko, Picasso, Pollock, Leger and other famous artists. Special stress is laid on the building up of a collection of the works of Israeli artists. Prints and drawings can be seen in the Graphic Halls. The Educational Service of the museum includes in its activities lecture tours for adults and guided tours for youngsters, as well as drawing, painting, graphic and sculpture classes.

123. Auguste Rodin (1840–1917, France) *The Head of Sorrow* (1882). Height 0.24 m. bronze
One of the bronzes of Rodin (see also pl. 100), complex and strong in its expression of human suffering.

124

125

126

124. The new building, Tel Aviv Museum
The sculpture in the foreground is **Henry Moore's** *Reclining Woman* (1969–70), one of his variations on this theme (for a later version see pl. 107; for an earlier work see pl. 145).

125. Entrance Hall and Main Staircase, Tel Aviv Museum
In the harmonious interior of the new building orientation is easy, the atmosphere serene. **Agam's** *Pace of Time* (see pl. XXXVI/176) to the right blends well with the interplay of the ramps facing the visitor.

126. Dizengoff House
The first building to house the Tel Aviv Museum was an enlargement of the private house of the city's first Mayor, Meir Dizengoff. It served the museum from 1931 to 1971.

129

127. Eugène Boudin (1824–1898, France) *Washerwomen*. 0.205 × 0.35 m. oil on wood

A characteristic picture of this forerunner of Impressionism, who dedicated most of his work to the painting of the waters and skies of France, the interplay of sea or river and the clouds above.

128. Camille Jacob Pissarro (1830–1903, France) *Street at Pontoise* (1867). 0.38 × 0.465 m. oil on canvas

This peaceful painting belongs to the French-Jewish artist's *plein-airist* period.

129. Jacques Lipchitz (1891–1973, France) *Dancer with Hood* (1947). Height 0.53 m. artificial stone

One variation of an important theme, of which the artist said: 'I was interested in the idea of the floating veil in its relationship to the twisting movement of the figure and the movement of her long braids of hair . . . *Dancer* is a highly complicated work in its movement in space, its organization in depth and in the variety of shapes.' (J. Lipchitz, *My Life in Sculpture*, London 1972, p. 178f.) (See also pl. 105.)

130. *Colour plate XV.* **James Ensor** (1860–1949, Belgium) *Ma Chambre préférée* (1892). 1 × 0.80 m. oil on canvas.

The museum is fortunate in having a choice collection of some fifteen paintings and drawings by this important Belgian artist, including one of his famous 'Masks'. The picture reproduced here has documentary importance, as it shows some of his own pictures, displayed in the artist's home.

131. *Colour plate XI.* **Paul Signac** (1865–1935, France) *St-Cloud*. 0.66 × 0.82 m. oil on canvas.

A typical example of Signac's Neo-Impressionist approach to painting.

132

133

132. Maurice Utrillo (1883–1955, France) *A Corner of Montmartre*. 0.30 × 0.45 m. oil on canvas
A characteristic picture by this artist (see pl. 89), showing a corner of his beloved Montmartre: at the right La Belle Gabrielle Café and the rue St Vincent.

134. *Colour plate XIX.* **Edouard Vuillard** (1868–1940, France) *The Model at Rest* (1910). 0.36 × 0.138 m. oil on canvas.
Vuillard painted only a very few nudes, preferring the dressed figure, and the decorative patterns of both dress and background. Some of the painter's uneasiness is reflected in the attitude of the nude model herself, who seems far from being at rest, in spite of the painting's title.

133. Alexander Archipenko (1887–1964, Russia) *Woman Powdering her Face* (1916). 0.85 × 0.65 m. oil on panel, painted relief construction in wood and metal
This Russian artist, who worked in Paris from 1908 and was one of the founders of Cubism, is well represented at the Tel Aviv Museum with some twenty works, of which this is an important example.

135. *Colour plate XX.* **Pierre Auguste Renoir** (1841–1919, France) *Nude*. 0.81 × 0.44 m. oil on canvas.
The young woman's body is beautifully and sensitively modelled, set in a landscape indicated in wide brush-strokes.

136. Edgar Degas (1834–1917, France) *Dancer Looking at the Sole of her Right Foot* (1910–11). Height 0.455 m. bronze
This is number fifty-nine of seventy-three sculptures cast in bronze between 1919 and 1921 from some one hundred and fifty surviving works in wax or clay created by Degas, many more having completely disintegrated. Twenty-two copies were made of each sculpture, marked with a capital letter, this one being marked 'J'. It belongs to a period when the master was nearly blind and had to check the details of the model's body with his hands. His passion, so well shown in this little statuette, was best expressed in Baudelaire's famous words, 'Degas loved the human body as material harmony and as beautiful architecture to which movement is added.'

137. Chana Orloff (1888–1968, Russia) *Mother and Child* (1924). Height 0.67 m. bronze

The Russian-born sculptor, a friend of Modigliani, Soutine and Pascin, must also be counted amongst the Jewish group of the Ecole de Paris. Her work is characterized by simplicity, dignity and tenderness.

138. *Colour plate XVIII.* **Kees van Dongen** (1877–1968, Holland) *Cabaret.* 0.66 × 0.82 m. oil on canvas.

In his special brand of Fauvism, van Dongen faithfully portrayed the twilight world of the aftermath of the First World War. Summing up the period, Maurice Rostand wrote:

'Nul n'aura comme toi su peindre cette
     époque
Si triste de plaisir et si vide d'amour.'

139. Amadeo Modigliani (1884–1920, Italy) *Caryatid.* 0.34 × 0.26 m. water-colour and pencil on paper

This is one of a number of sculptures, paintings and drawings of Caryatids which Modigliani created between 1912 and 1917. In these, as in all his work, form is only one means of expressing feeling, both of the model and the artist. He had dreamed of building a temple to humanity, surmounted by hundreds of these Caryatids. Modigliani, son of a Jewish-Italian family which traced its ancestry back to Spinoza, died very young, having lived as he had wished, 'a short, but intensive life'.

137

140

124

140. Juan Gris (1887–1927, Spain) *La Jolie* (1921). 0.33 × 0.55 m. oil on canvas
Born in Spain, this artist went to Paris in 1910. In the framework of his Synthetic Cubism, he aimed at the creation of a new reality, a poetic approach towards inanimate objects: a newspaper, fruit, vessels

141. Maurice de Vlaminck (1876–1958, France) *Village at Dusk*. 0.65 × 0.75 m. oil on canvas
One of the leaders of the Fauves, his work is well represented by this typical painting. The strong movement of the roads and clouds clearly express the painter's dynamism.

142. Ossip Zadkine (1890–1967, France) *Head of a Man*. Height 0.32 m. bronze
The compact image of this head expresses, in clear-cut geometric forms, the dignity of man. One of the Jewish group of the Ecole de Paris, Zadkine was destined to survive two world wars and the Holocaust and to create monumental works expressing the horror, the heroism, and the eternal protest. At Rotterdam harbour his monument stands in memory of that brave city's agony (see also pl. 104).

143. *Colour plate XVI.* **Chaim Soutine** (1894–1944, Russia) *Landscape at Cagnes*. 0.63 × 0.90 m. oil on canvas.
This Russian-born Jewish painter of the Ecole de Paris expressed the pain and restlessness within himself through the violent motion of the subject itself.

144. *Colour plate XXI.* **Marc Chagall** (born 1887, Russia) *Jew with Torah*. 0.68 × 0.51 m. gouache on paper.
One of a select group of works of this great artist, exhibited at the museum. A number of similar gouaches, showing Jews in their snowy exile, were done by Chagall in 1930 (see also pl. 246).

142

146

145. Henry Moore (born 1898, England) *Figure with Clasped Hands* (1929). Height 0.457 m. travertine
This sculpture belongs to Moore's early work, when, as he puts it, he had 'slight Cubist tendencies'. It is a good starting-point for a study of his work, other examples of which may be seen in the Tel Aviv Museum (see pl. 124) and elsewhere in the country (see pl. 107).

146. Umberto Boccioni (1882–1916, Italy) *Self portrait*. 0.46 × 0.38 m. oil on canvas
An interesting picture of a major founder and leader of Futurism, express-ing something of the painter's inner tension and urge for constant action.

147

147. Jackson Pollock (1912–1966, USA) *Prisms* (1947). 0.41 × 0.46 m. oil on canvas

One of America's 'action-painters', Pollock did these paintings by dripping and flinging paint on the canvas, creating the work through and out of his body's movements.

148

148. Ziona Tagger (born 1900, Israel) *Sitting Girl* (1927). 0.60 × 0.50 m. oil on canvas

Modern Israel's first native-born painter, Ziona Tagger studied in Jerusalem and Paris. Upon her return to the country in 1925, she became one of the first modernists amongst local painters.

149. *Colour plate XXIII.* **Max Ernst** (born 1891, France) *La Planète Affolée* (1942). 1.10 × 1.40 m. oil on canvas.

Ernst moved from Dada to Surrealism and this picture still carries traces of the former. Parts of it are executed in a technique called 'decalcomania'—the squashing of wet paint on the canvas, in order to convey the impression of decay. To this Ernst here added the technique of 'dripping': paint drips from a hole in a can, swung in regular motion over the canvas.

150

150. Jacob Epstein (1880–1959, England) *Princess Menan* (1949). Height 0.67 m. bronze
During her stay in London this half-Belgian niece of the Empress of Ethiopia sat for the famous British artist of American-Jewish origin.

151

151. **Zeev Ben-Zvi** (1904–1952, Poland) *Portrait of Shmaryahu Levin* (1934). Height 0.53 m. stone
Ben-Zvi started his art studies in Poland and continued them in 1924 at the Bezalel Art School in Jerusalem; in 1936 he became one of its first teachers. His work, mainly portraits, is conceived on Cubist principles, executed in stone and bronze. The portrait of Shmaryahu Levin (1867–1935), Zionist leader, writer and publicist, is characteristic of both the artist's and the model's forceful personalities.

152. Moshe Mokadi (born 1902, Poland) *Violinist* (1949). 0.81 × 0.65 m. oil on canvas

Having studied painting and music in Vienna and Zurich, Mokadi came to Palestine in 1920. From 1927 to 1932 he worked in Paris, where he was strongly influenced by the Jewish painters of the Ecole de Paris. His ardent emotions, his deep love of music and form are well expressed in this painting.

153. Reuben Rubin (born 1893, Romania) *Family of the Artist* (1927). 1.63 × 1.29 m. oil on canvas

Another aspect of this artist's early work. (See also pl. XIV/95).

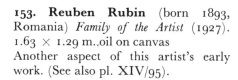
152

153

154. *Colour plate XXXV.* **Marcel Janco** (born 1895, Romania) *Turnavitu* (1968). 0.73 × 1 m. oil on canvas.

Janco, originally an architect, studied art in Zurich. He was one of the early Dadaists; though he left this movement after a time, he has never completely lost touch with it. Living in the country since 1941, Janco founded the artists' village of En Hod, south of Haifa, in 1953.

155. *Colour plate XXIV.* **Fernand Léger** (1881–1955, France) *Flowers* (1954). 0.73 × 0.92 m. oil on canvas.

It is interesting to compare this picture with one done by the artist thirty years earlier (see pl. 87). The painter has remained true to his fundamental approach to art, though this has mellowed with maturity.

156

156. Israel Paldi (born 1892, Russia)
Night Story (1960–1963). 0.73 × 1.30 m.
oil and collage on canvas
Paldi came to Palestine in 1909, but
studied art in Europe from 1910 to 1920.
This naïve painting is characteristic of
Paldi's very individual approach to art.

157

157. Yeheskiel Streichman (born
1906, Lithuania) *Portrait of a Woman*
(1951). 1.30 × 0.97 m. oil on canvas
Streichman started his studies in Jerusalem in 1926. In 1948 he was one of
the founders of the 'New Horizons'
group, among whom were Castel,
Kahana, Janco, Zaritsky, Mairovich
and Stematsky (*q.v.*). The painting reproduced here is typical of Streichman's
work of the fifties, his later paintings
becoming abstract.

158. *Colour plate XXII.* **Oskar Kokoschka** (born 1886, Czechoslovakia) *Saul
and David* (1966). 1 × 1.30 m. oil on
canvas.
This Expressionist painter grew up in
Austria and travelled widely before
making his home in England. He finally
settled in Switzerland. In the Biblical
story of Saul and David he found an
expression of his innermost self: 'They
both embody the primaeval powers of
my life.' About this picture the artist
also said: 'Look at this figure Saul—he
has a tremendous grudge against his
age. He is furious at being eighty—as I
am. He cannot grasp the fact that he is
now eighty, as yesterday he was only
eighteen—like David who is standing
behind him in this picture—it seems
only yesterday I was eighteen . . .'
(Marlborough Catalogue, *Kokoschka*,
London, 1969, p. 7).

159. Arie Aroch (born 1908, Russia) *Bus in the Mountains.* 0.70 m. oil on canvas. See p. 84 for further details about this artist.

159

160

160. Yossl Bergner (born 1920, Austria) *Woman at the Window* (1956). 0.81 × 0.65 m. oil on canvas
Vienna-born son of a Yiddish poet, Bergner grew up in Poland and moved to Australia in 1937. From there he went to Israel in 1951. Bergner and Bak (pl. XXV/177) should be considered Israel's chief representatives of Surrealism.

161. *Colour plate XXVII.* **Menahem Shemi** (1897–1951, Russia) *Safed Landscape.* 0.46 × 0.60 m. oil on canvas.
Having arrived in the country as a child, Shemi became one of the first students of the Jerusalem Bezalel Art School to revolt against the academism ruling there at the time. He became one of the country's most important modernists, evolving an independent and vigorous style, which yet expresses the poetry of the Galilean landscape.

162

163

164

162. Mordechai Levanon (1901–68, Romania) *King Solomon's Pillars* (1959). 0.92 × 0.72 m. oil on canvas
Levanon came to Palestine as a young man, studying art locally. He became one of Israel's Expressionists, depicting the landscape of his country, its ancient majesty and its mystic message in strong colours and forms.

163. Yehiel Krize (1809–1968, Poland) *Into Space* 1 × 0.70 m. gouache on cardboard
Krize came to Tel Aviv in 1924, starting work as a weaver. Self-taught, he mainly painted landscapes. Between 1955 and 1963 he turned to the abstract. His aims in paintings such as the one reproduced here is best summed up in his own words: 'With time I spanned the space, made my painting more silent and essential in its expression'.

164. Moshe Ziffer (born 1902, Poland) *Sculpture* (1961). Height 0.72 m. bronze
Ziffer came to Palestine in 1919. Between the two world wars he studied art in Europe. Until the late fifties a figurative sculptor, he then turned to abstract work. Our picture shows an early example of the latter.

165. Arieh Lubin (born 1897, USA)
Hookah Smokers (1959). 0.455 × 0.55 m.
oil on canvas
Lubin enrolled in 1913 as a pupil in
Tel Aviv's first Hebrew high-school.
Having studied art in the United States,
he returned to Tel Aviv in 1923. He
draws local landscapes and figures in
geometric forms, though he remains
essentially a figurative painter.

165

166. Buki Schwartz (born 1932, Jerusalem) *Red Sculpture* (1963). Height 2 m.
painted steel
Schwartz studied art in Tel Aviv and
at the St Martin's School of Art,
London, where he also taught. His work
is strongly influenced by recent English
sculptors.

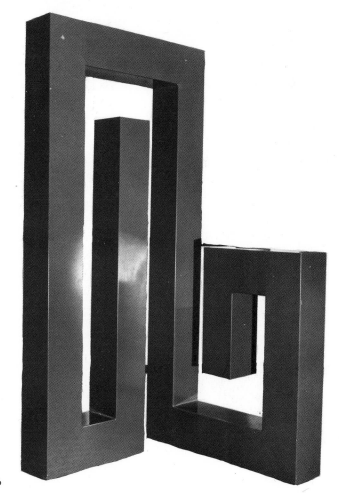

166

167. Avigdor Arikha (born 1929, Romania) *Saccades* (1964). 1.46 × 1.14 m. oil on canvas
Arikha did his first work as an artist in a Romanian concentration-camp in the years 1941–1944; he then went to Jerusalem and studied there and later in Paris. He has since divided his time between the two cities. The painting reproduced here is a good example of the artist's abstract work, expressing, as its title implies, 'Sudden Movement'.

168. Moshe Castel (born 1909, Jerusalem) *Manuscript from Canaan.* 1.62 × 3.43 m. pulverized basalt and oil on canvas
Castel lived and studied for many years in Paris, settling in Safed in 1940. Moving from Expressionism to the Abstract, he has in the last decade turned for inspiration to locally found antiquities: steles, inscriptions, ancient manuscripts.

169. *Colour plate XXX.* **Aharon Kahana** (1905–1967, Germany) *The Pianist* (1966). 1.30 × 0.81 m. oil on canvas.
Kahana studied art in Germany and France, coming to Palestine in 1934. He has moved from Abstract to pop and poster art, of which this picture is an example. He also uses ceramics as a medium.

167

168

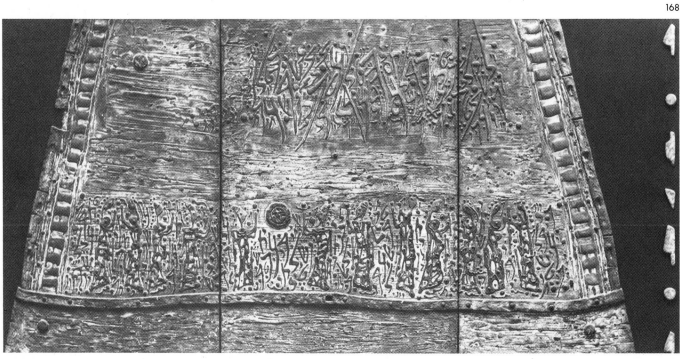

170. Zvi Mairovich (born 1911, Poland) *Painting* (1970). 1 × 1 m. mixed media on paper
Mairovich came to Haifa in 1935 via Berlin and Paris, where he studied art. His abstract paintings have changed since the sixties both in media and approach.

171. Jacob Wexler (born 1912, Latvia) *Wheels* (1968). 1.31 × 0.92 m. oil on canvas
Wexler turned from Expressionism to the Abstract. This picture is one of a group exploring the stress of wheels in motion.

172. *Colour plate XXXI.* **Lea Nikel** (born 1918, Russia) *Painting* (1969). 0.89 × 1.16 m. oil on canvas.
Living in Palestine since infancy, Lea Nikel has studied art locally under Stematsky (pl. 178) and Streichman (pl. 157). This abstract picture is representative of her work, which is dominated by strong colours.

171

170

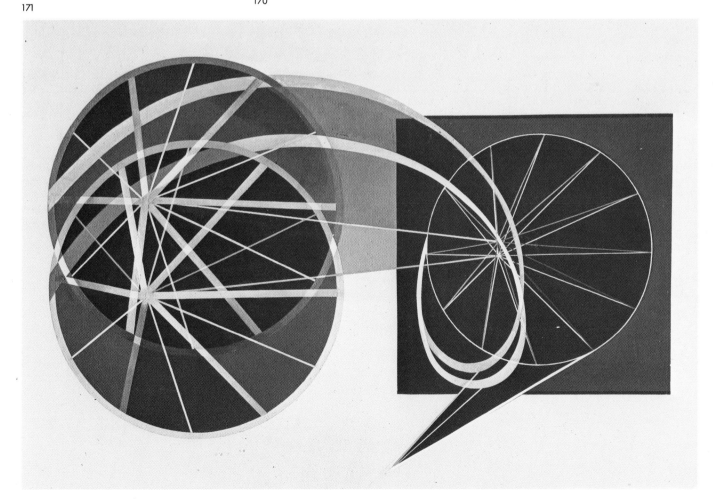

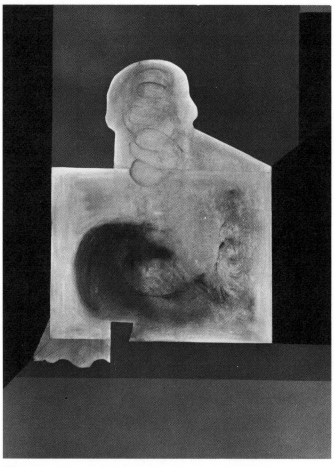

173

174

173. Moshe Givati (born 1934, Palestine) *Portrait* (1968). 1.40 × 1.30 m. oil on canvas

Locally trained, Givati is one of the many painters who are or were members of Israel's kibbutzim. He expresses himself in strong abstract forms.

176. *Colour plate XXXVI.* **Yaacov Agam** (born 1928, Israel) *Pace of Time* (1970). 4.20 × 6.30 m. painted aluminium relief.

Agam studied in Jerusalem and Paris. The Jewish mystical concepts of the Deity, acquired from childhood by this son of a rabbi, have remained the main source of his work: 'One Being, yet unique in unity'. To express this concept, Agam created works of art in different media, which he classified as Transformable Paintings, Tactiles, and Polyphonic Pictures. To be fully appreciated this work must be viewed from many angles. (See also pl. 125.)

174. Jean David (born 1908, Romania) *Girl-Dove* (1970). 0.92 × 0.73 m. acrylic on canvas

After having studied in France, David was for many years a seaman, serving in the years 1944–1947 in the British Navy and in 1949–50 in the Israeli Navy. David's paintings and graphic works, at times using ancient motifs, express emotion of love and also a gentle humour.

177. *Colour plate XXV.* **Shmuel Bak** (born 1933, Lithuania) *Portrait* (1970). 0.65 × 0.46 m. oil on canvas.

Bak survived the horrors of the Nazi camps, coming to Israel in 1948. He studied art in Jerusalem, Paris and Rome and was strongly influenced by modern Italian art. As he has said, his surrealist canvases are 'an expression of moods, impressions and recollections'.

175. *Colour plate XXXIV.* **Joseph Zaritsky** (born 1891, Russia) *Landscape.* 0.46 × 0.55 m. oil on canvas.

This painting is a variation of the artist's 'Yehiam' series, which started in 1954–55 with paintings of the castle at Kibbutz Yehiam in Western Galilee. (See also pl. 91.)

178. *Colour plate XXXIII.* **Avigdor Stematsky** (born 1908, Russia) *Echoes of Childhood* (1970). 1.30 × 1 m. oil on canvas.

Having come in infancy to Palestine, Stematsky studied art in Jerusalem and Paris. Since 1948 he has developed an abstract style, of which our picture is a recent lyrical example.

179.

179. Yohanan Simon (born 1906, Germany) *Euphoric Composition* (1971). 1 × 0.72 m. oil on canvas
Simon studied art in Germany and France, coming to Palestine in 1936. He travelled extensively through Europe and South America. Images in his paintings, like the one here reproduced, are reminiscent of the latter's tropical vegetation.

180. Pinchas Eshet (born 1935, Romania) *Genesis* (1969). Height 1 m. bronze, chrome-plated
Eshet came to Israel after the Second World War. He studied art locally and continued his studies under Marino Marini in Italy. He returned to Israel in 1962.

180

181

181. Uri Lifshitz (born 1936, Israel) *Schizophrene.* 0.89 × 1.16 m. oil on canvas

Representative of the 'new figuration' in contemporary Israeli art, Lifshitz brings a highly disturbing element to the local artistic scene, similar in some respects to that brought to the European art world by Francis Bacon.

182. Yigael Tumarkin (born 1933, Germany) *Crusader Kingdom* (1971). Height 0.65 m. length 1.31 m. stainless steel and iron

Brought to Palestine in early childhood, Tumarkin studied in Europe between 1955 and 1961. He has since developed his very personal style, juxtaposing symbols, abstract forms and scrap-metal. This work is one of a group, some of which are exhibited in the Crusader halls recently cleared under Acre's citadel.

183. *Colour plate XXXVII.* **Nachum Gutman** (born 1899, Romania) *On the Jaffa Road* (1971). 0.81 × 1 m. oil on canvas.

Living in Palestine since childhood, Gutman became one of Israel's interpretative painters, especially of his country's landscapes of the twenties. He wrote and illustrated *Little Tel Aviv: A Little City and Few Men Within It*, a book about the city's early days, written in 1959. Both his paintings and his children's illustrated tales reveal his gentle humour.

182

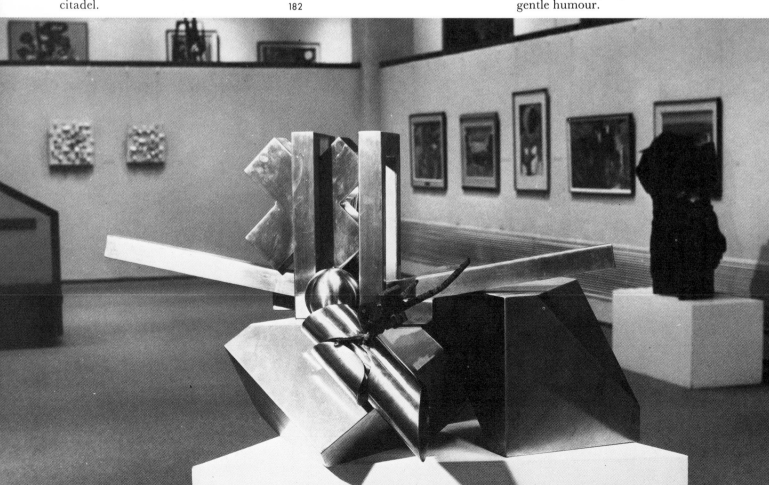

184

THE HA'ARETZ MUSEUM

This museum (lit. 'the museum of the land') was founded in 1953 by the late Dr Walter Moses who left to the city his important collection of ancient and modern glass and pottery, to form the nucleus of a Municipal Museum complex, opened in the Ramat Aviv suburb in 1958. **The Glass Pavilion** displays all the ancient methods of glass-making and exhibits beautiful examples of early Egyptian (1500 BC) and Phoenician glass, made long before the glass-blowing process was known. There follows a rich collection of blown-glass—probably a Sidonian invention—from the first century BC onwards. One of the museum's finest examples of such glass comes from this region. The exhibition displays beautiful examples of some of the fantastic shapes given to glass vessels—fruits, heads and animals—as well as of the different uses to which glass was put; the display includes some rare Jewish glasses—both vessels and jewellery, decorated with the Menorah. A fine collection of Islamic as well as European glass, brings us to recent times.

The Ceramics Pavilion, opened in 1966, shows in a similar manner a comprehensive picture of pottery-making in antiquity, enlarging its exhibit with interesting parallels from present African and South American techniques. It demonstrates the different uses of ceramics—from kitchen-ware to beautifully decorated Cypriot and Greek vases, from figurines used in cults or for aesthetic enjoyment to the use of clay tablets as writing material. A systematic display shows the development of pottery forms found in excavations in this country. A reconstruction of a dwelling of the time of the Judaean Monarchy is attached to this museum to show the use of the pottery of that period in the different parts of the household. The courtyard displays a number of showcases used for temporary exhibitions—very often of local artists in the field of ceramics. The mural by one of these artists stands at the entrance of the pavilion.

The **Kadman Numismatic Pavilion**, opened in 1962, contains the founder's fine collection of Jewish and Palestinian coins, to which much important material has since been added. Besides the demonstration of the development of primitive and early money, and the processes of minting, this museum displays a complete set of the coins and paper money of Israel, either minted or printed here.

The **Metallurgy Pavilion** was added in 1971 to form the nucleus of a future section of the museum. It has finds from excavations in the Arabah, where Edomites and perhaps also Midianites worked coppermines, not later than the eleventh century BC.

The **Museum of Ethnography and Folklore**, opened in 1963, was founded by local groups interested in Jewish folk-art and costumes. It shows groups of models clothed in costumes from all over the world, wherever the Jews settled, demonstrating such occasions as the marriage ceremonies of Oriental Jewish communities or the kindling of the Shabbat lights in an Eastern European Jewish home. Also on permanent view are collections of Jewish ceremonial art, marriage-contracts and manuscripts. The museum has now been enhanced by the reconstruction of an Italian synagogue of the eighteenth century.

The **Adam ve'Amalo** (lit. 'Man and his work') collection is now being transferred from its present cramped premises to this museum's campus. Tools and implements exemplify indigenous work-methods,

185. Mosque Lamp (fourteenth century) unknown provenance. Height 0.40 m. enamelled and gilded glass
Such lamps were made in Damascus for the Mamluk Sultans and Emirs in Cairo. This lamp carries Arabic inscriptions with quotations from the Koran, XXIV:35: 'God is the light of Heaven and the Earth, His light is as a niche in which is a lamp', and the dedication, mentioning an Emir under the sultans Al Nasir ibn Qualawun and one of his sons, Al Hasan, in the first half of the fourteenth century. According to his coat-of-arms, he was cup-bearer (*Săqî*) to the sultans.

186

186. Geula Ogen, *Pottery* (1966). Length 6.50 m. Height 2.50 m. terracotta
This wall-relief, made of unglazed terracotta tiles, shows the main pottery-making processes: from the preparation of the clay (centre) to the building-up of a vessel with clay-coils (right) or clay being thrown on the potter's wheel (upper right); finally, its firing (far left). Geula Ogen is a well-known local potter; her terracotta wall-reliefs grace several public buildings in the country.

both in agriculture and in industry, showing the uses of manual labour, animals, water-power and more modern sources of energy. The large items will be installed as an open-air exhibition in the museum's park.

The Alphabet Museum, founded by one of the foremost experts in the development of writing and the alphabet, Professor D. Diringer, shows this fundamental form of communication most fittingly in a country which may indeed, in company with its neighbours, Lebanon and North-West Syria, be regarded as the cradle of the twenty-four-letter Semitic alphabet still used to this day.

The Museum of Science and Technology is, at the time this book goes to print, building a new pavilion near the museum's **Planetarium.** A large display of working models will show visitors, especially young people, the theoretical and practical background to the fundamentals of science and technology. This approach gives to the Ha'aretz Museum its special and valuable flavour. Each pavilion is dedicated to one basic material—glass, ceramics or metal, or to the use of written communication or monetary exchange; the many beautiful and rare examples enable the visitor, and especially the student, to understand the subject from many angles.

In addition to these pavilions on the Ha'aretz Museum's main site at Ramat Aviv, it also administers two historic museums, each

187

located at a site suitable to its contents: **The Museum of Antiquities of Tel Aviv/Jaffa** is established in a spacious Turkish house of the nineteenth century, near the ancient site of the city of Jaffa. Exhibited in the beautiful vaulted rooms are some of the valuable finds from the region, ranging from neolithic figurines and Canaanite pottery and weapons, to relics of Egyptian imperial rule in this city such as the royal inscriptions of Ramses II on its gate-posts (it was probably in this ruler's time that the Exodus of the Children of Israel from Egypt took place). The exhibition includes finds from Hasmonean fortifications and Herodian tombs, down to Byzantine and early Arab times. Nearby, some of the layers of this site's excavations may be inspected, including the city's glacis in use from the seventeenth century BC to 701 BC.

The Museum of the History of Tel Aviv has recently been transferred to a most appropriate location: the old municipality building in Bialik Square. Besides the reconstructed offices of this city's first mayor, in this Museum one may understand something of that 'Little Tel Aviv' which existed only some fifty years ago, and learn about its quick development into the present modern city.

A unique feature of the Ha'aretz Museum on its Ramat Aviv campus is the major archaeological site—Tel Qasile—actually under excavation. Already unearthed and partly reconstructed are Judaean houses of the ninth to eighth centuries BC and a Philistine temple of the eleventh century BC, which existed until the days of King David.

to p.154

187. Fertility Figurines
This display exhibits the wide range in time, execution and technique in the making of these terracotta figurines in the Eastern Mediterranean. From left to right:

Judaean Pillar-Figurine (seventh century BC). Height 0.16 m. mould-made head attached to handmade body. While the moulds were brought in from Phoenicia, the body was made by the local Judaean potter.

Two Canaanite 'Bird-Face' Figurines (fourteenth to thirteenth century BC). Heights 0.17 and 0.13 m. Handmade figurines appeared mainly in Lebanon and Syria. The holes in the ears often hold metal earrings.

Back row: **Enthroned Figurine** (Beginning seventh century BC). Height 0.13 m. handmade, probably from Greece.

Mycenaean Figurine (fourteenth to thirteenth century BC). Height 0.14 m. handmade, painted red and black.

Red-polished Cypriot Figurine (third millennium BC). Height 0.18 m. handmade, incised decoration on flat body.

to p.153

XXII. **Oskar Kokoschka,** *Saul and David.* Tel Aviv Museum. (Note 158)

XXXIII. **Avigdor Stematsky,** *Echoes of Childhood*, 1970. Tel Aviv Museum. (Note 178)

Cypriot Figurine (sixth century BC). Height 0.35 m. mouldmade.

While most of these figurines seem to represent a female deity, the last one may also represent the deity's priestess, perhaps personifying the goddess. All these figurines may at different times have served different purposes: actual representations of the Great Mother, for veneration at home; figurines for use in some magic ceremonial to assure fertility and abundance for the living, and for life in the tomb; or as rather superficially used fertility—or even apotropaic—amulets. They were probably used mainly in the latter capacity by Judaeans of the seventh to sixth centuries BC, and thus do not seem to have worried the prophets overmuch, who fought against the worship of the major Canaanite gods. These figurines seem to have been derided collectively under the abusive name *Teraphim* (lit. 'vile things') used in the Bible for such statuettes, though not necessarily exclusively for the female ones. (See also pl. 38.)

188. Mother Figurine (third century AD). Height 0.19 m. mouldmade, terracotta

This figurine seems to have originated in one of the workshops in the Judaean mountains, perhaps at Bet Natif, which yielded many examples of statuettes of this style. It has two main characteristics: it is apparently eyeless since the original paint, indicating the eyes, has worn off; and it is completely frontal. This frontality was to influence Byzantine and European Pre-Romanesque art. The figurine probably still represents a fertility-goddess, a giver of children and their protectress.

189. *Colour plate XXXVIII.* **The Ennion Jug** (first century AD) unknown provenance. Height (including handle) 0.22 m. glass.

This very fine jug of dark blue glass, blown in a three-part mould, carries in its central frieze a framed Greek inscription, which reads: 'Ennion made me'. Only two more jugs of this type, probably from the same mould, are recorded: one in the Metropolitan Museum of Art, and the other in the Corning Museum—both in the USA. Ennion is known to have been a Phoenician glass-maker. Only two others to date are known by name. The jug is said to have been found originally in Jerusalem, where indeed recent excavations unearthed fragments of a similar vessel.

188

190

190. Pottery Wheels
The only reconstructed items among these fairly simple instruments for the manufacture of wheel-made pottery of excellent finish are the wooden wheel-heads. These are fastened to the pivot, which turns in a socket (diam. *c.* 0.16 m.), originally held either by an assistant or fastened to a base, probably also of wood; a lubricant speeded the turning. The wheels on the right belong to the Canaanite period of the seventeenth to thirteenth centuries BC), those on the left to the Byzantine period (sixth century AD). The latter by their height give greater stability when throwing the vessel. But for this small improvement, the method seems to have worked perfectly for over two thousand years.

This temple has yielded a rich find of Philistine pottery, including unique cult-vessels. Further levels on the site continue to the sixth century AD. Excavations on this site will prove worthwhile for many years in the future.

The educational services of the Museum stress the creative aspects of the children's activities, having already achieved very interesting results in this field.

191. Tetradrachm of Bar Kokhba
(AD 134–5). Diam. 0.025 m. silver
A coin struck in the last year of the
short period of the Jews' second war
against Rome (AD 132–135). The front
of the temple is shown on the coin, a
star above the architrave. On both sides,
written in Hebrew is the name *Shim'on*,
the first name of Bar Kokhba. The
reverse shows the palm branch and
citrus fruit, used in Temple-services on
the Feast of Tabernacles, and the
Hebrew inscription 'For the Freedom
of Jerusalem'. Both the representation
of the Temple and the emphasis on
Jerusalem, at that time out of reach of
fighters reduced to mountain hide-outs
and desert caves, reminds one of the
'Jerusalem' inscription of 701 BC in a
Judaean tomb-cave, expressing an
identical sentiment in a similar situation (see pl. 37).

192. The Noah Coin (AD 244–249).
Diam. 0.034 m. bronze
This type of coin was struck in Apamea
on the Meander river, in Phrygia (Asia
Minor) under Roman Emperors of the
first half of the third century AD, as was
this specimen, under Philippus Arabus.
The coin shows Noah and his wife in the
Ark, with the Greek letters NOE inscribed on its side. Above appear the
raven and the dove with the olive twig.
To the left Noah and his wife are
repeated, standing on firm ground and
thanking the Lord with uplifted hands.
The inscription carries the names of the
local priests, under whom the coin was
struck. Even though Phrygia had its
own flood legends, perhaps evolved
from great antiquity, independant of
Jewish tradition, the representation
identifying Noah by name must surely
have been influenced by local Jewish
concepts; perhaps copied from a synagogue mural or an illuminated Bible
manuscript.

193. Jewish Renaissance Medal
(1503). Diam. 0.0175 m. bronze
This cast medal carries a long Hebrew
inscription mentioning Benjamin ben
Eliyah Be'er, the physician, who lived
under Pope Julius II in Rome. It is
not known whom the head, subscribed
with the word UMILITAS, represents,
nor has the inscription been fully
deciphered. This is the earliest Jewish
medal known.

194

194. Tell Qasile's Philistine Temple
(mid-eleventh century BC)

The site of Tell Qasile is located inside the grounds of the Ha'aretz Museum. The site, on the banks of the Yarkon river, contains Judaean houses of the ninth to eighth centuries BC; under these a Philistine settlement was revealed which came into existence in the twelfth century BC with the entry of this and other 'sea-peoples' into the country. A Philistine temple was the major find of this excavation, which is likely to continue for many years.

Even though part of the current excavation has now sunk below the temple floor, one can still make out the original floor-plan. The temple, built of mudbricks, has an over-all measurement of 14.5 × 8 m. Entrance and stone threshold are right foreground, the entrance-room, with benches along its inner walls, centre-foreground. The broad entrance to the main sanctuary (measuring 7.20 × 5.65 m.) is slightly to the right, the altar opposite, and also has benches around its inner walls. The round object to the left of the altar is one of two stone bases originally carrying wooden columns which held up the roof; the second one was attached to the left side of the altar. The distance between the columns was about 1.90 m. It was destroyed in a fierce fire at the beginning of the tenth century BC. So

156

far this is the only temple of any 'sea-people', possibly Philistines, to have been discovered. The two main columns of the edifice, standing in rather close proximity, remind one of the description of such a temple's destruction: 'And Samson took hold of the two middle pillars upon which the house stood, and on which it was borne up, of the one with his right hand, and of the one with his left. And Samson said: Let me die with the Philistines. And he bowed himself with all his might; and the house fell upon the lords, and upon all the people that were therein.' (Jud. 16:29–30).

195. Tell Qasile Excavations (mid-eleventh century BC)
The photograph (left) shows excavation in progress in part of of the temple's storerooms, some of the large storage jars still standing as left at the time of the temple's destruction.

196. Museum of Antiquities of Tel Aviv, Jaffa
The museum was opened in 1951 in a nineteenth-century Turkish house. It stands at the foot of the ancient site of Jaffa, now partly excavated, and includes occupation levels from the eighteenth to the first centuries BC.

197. *Colour plate XL.* **Marriage-Deed** (1776) North Italy. 0.79 × 0.63 m. parchment
The Jewish marriage-deed (*Ketubbah*), is drawn up in Aramaic, the common language of large parts of the Jewish people in the first centuries AD. The text, formulated at that time, states the financial and social obligations of the bridegroom towards his future wife, ensuring her rights in marriage and, in case of divorce, specifying the indemnities and return of dowry due to her in the latter event. The document is read out in full at the marriage ceremony, the attendants serving as public witnesses. This being a document dedicated to a joyful occasion, it became customary to have it illuminated. In these documents too we witness the general trend of Jewish ceremonial art, to adopt the style of the country and period in which the Jews found themselves at the time.

198. Philistine Cult Vessels (mid-eleventh century BC)
These two vessels come from the temple described in pls. 194–5. The offering-stand to the right (height 0.45 m.) would originally have served to support a dish holding the actual sacrifice. Its decoration shows four figurines in profile advancing to the left, hands raised, in what may be a ceremonial dance. The dish nearby has the head, wings and tail of a bird, probably a duck.

198

199

199. Kindling the Shabbat Lights (end nineteenth century) Poland
This reconstruction of a Jewish home somewhere in Poland evokes the moment when the housewife ushers in the Shabbat with the kindling of the lights, one of the three fundamental duties of the Jewish wife (see pl. 68). Set on a special tray (see pl. 220), the braided wheat-loaves are covered with a richly embroidered cloth (see pl. VI/78). The housewife wears her feast-day dress. Her head is covered with an embroidered head-dress instead of the weekday kerchief. To her benediction, praising the Lord, who 'advised us to kindle the Light of Shabbat' she will traditionally add her private prayers for the life and health of her beloved ones. Soon her husband will return with their sons from the synagogue. Before starting the Shabbat meal with the benediction over wine (see pl. 69) and bread, he will intone the two ancient songs, which exemplify to the Jewish house the spirit of Shabbat. The first bestows greetings of peace and welcome to the Angels of the Almighty, King of Kings, the Holy One; the second song takes its text from Proverbs 31:10–31, praising the virtuous and industrious woman, mistress of the home.

200. The Gate of Ramses II (1290–1224 BC) Jaffa

Standing before photos of this ruler's mummy and statue are parts of the gateposts of the city of Jaffa, carrying his name and his official titles. This gate, three metres wide, and the city which it defended, were found under a burned layer, witness to the destruction perpetrated by the 'sea-peoples' who invaded the eastern Mediterranean coasts at this period.

200

201

201. Museum of the History of Tel Aviv

This museum is housed in Tel Aviv's old municipality building and administered by the Ha'aretz Museum. The building shown here is one of the few surviving houses of 'little Tel Aviv'. It was opened in 1925 as a hotel, but became a municipality building in 1927, serving the city until 1966 when it became a museum. The old building and the houses surrounding the square in front of it evoke memories of the early days of a small town, when all the inhabitants still knew each other, and a stroll to this spot and then to the seashore was sufficient Shabbat entertainment. Some of the vanished atmosphere of those days has been caught in the exhibitions in this museum, which was opened to the public in 1971.

THE MUSEUMS
OF HAIFA

Founded in the 1950s and early 1960s, Haifa's municipal museums are housed in various parts of the city. Many of them started from private collections, and for most the exhibition space available is now insufficient. Only one can be called either adequate or modern but the others hope to obtain a central building to exhibit their collections in the foreseeable future. **The Museums of Ancient and Modern Art** are both squeezed into a side-wing of the Municipality building of the city. The former had to store most of its fine collection of antiquities, mostly Greek and Roman, much of it local, as well as a good collection of Egypto-Roman portraits. Instead, it shows the finds from the interesting local site of Shikmona, ranging from the tenth century BC to the Byzantine and early Arab periods. **The**

202

160

THE MUSEUM OF ANCIENT ART

202. Tomb Door (fourth to fifth centuries AD) Tamra (Western Galilee). Height 1.35 m. stone
The lintel is decorated with stylized shells and a Menorah in its centre; the posts carry representations of jars, topped by a peacock and a partridge respectively. The heavy stone door, turning on stone hinges, is fashioned to simulate a wooden panelled door, with metal corner-straps and another Menorah in its upper centre. Such doors, more or less decorated, are common in Jewish tombs of the Roman period, especially in the north of the country (see pl. 227). It is difficult to assert a symbolic meaning for the representation of the birds on the vases, so different from contemporary Christian representations of birds (symbolizing human souls) drinking from a vessel (symbolizing eternal life).

203. Phoenician Mask (ninth to eighth century BC) Achsib. Height 0.13 m. terracotta
Both male and female masks have been found in a number of Phoenician tombs, in Achsib as well as in other Phoenician settlements, as far away as North Africa. All are too small to have been worn. Some still have traces of paint, as has this one, representing a dignified, bearded man; red colour adheres to the ears and black to the hair. At its top the small mask has a suspension-hole. Both this and the size leave no doubt that such masks were not actually worn, but suspended. They may either have been intended to serve both the living and the dead, as amulets against all evil influences or they may have represented deities.

204. Servant Girl (tenth to ninth century BC) Achsib. Height 0.19 m. terracotta
The figurine's body is painted red and has a yellow band round the loins, while a blue and yellow necklace is painted round the neck. All this, together with the heavy wig surmounted by a perfume-cone, is in the Egyptian style, though the workmanship is Phoenician, as is the tomb where it was found. The image was probably intended as a consort for the deceased. (For other Phoenician figurines, most of a later date, see pls. 38–9.)

204

161

205

Museum of Modern Art stores most of its permanent collection of local paintings and graphics in order to allow the public to see frequent temporary exhibitions. **The Museum of Prehistory** shows a permanent exhibition of the prehistoric finds in the Carmel mountain range, using dioramas and other visual aids in its display.

The Music Museum includes a collection of very important archives pertaining to music connected with the Bible and biblical themes, as well as themes connected with Jewish composers and their music. The exhibits include local representations or reconstructions of ancient musical instruments and also those from abroad.

The Ethnological Museum, in its very cramped quarters, is scarcely able to exhibit. Its main and important work centres around its Israel folklore archives.

The National Maritime Museum opened its modern and spacious halls to the public in 1973. Close to the sea, it exhibits a broad and detailed picture of maritime activities, mainly Mediterranean, from antiquity to modern times. The many original items are supplemented by excellent models, demonstrating in detail ships

NATIONAL MARITIME MUSEUM

205. Funerary Supply-Boat (nineteenth century BC) Egypt. Length 0.99 m. wood

Models of boats which served the living for journeys on the Nile, were put into Egyptian tombs, in accordance with the belief in an after-life in the nether-world. This model, showing a group of servants and supplies, must be one of a number of such model-boats, put into the master's tomb; often as many as twelve boats have been found in one tomb, including travelling and supply boats, fishing- and fowling-skiffs and the funerary barque. This boat is shown against the museum's façade, which carries a large bronze relief by G. Knispel.

206. Maritime Aphrodite (third century BC). Height 0.33 m. terracotta

This charming Hellenistic representation of Aphrodite taking off a sandal to enter her bath emphasizes her maritime character by using a steering-oar as her support. Aphrodite, born from the foam of the sea, either at Cythera or on the Syrian coast and washed ashore at Cyprus, was at all times venerated by mariners. It is possible that this was a Greek interpretation of the much older concept of the mighty goddess of the Canaanite merchant-sailors, Asherat-Yam, 'Asherah-of-the-Sea' (see pl. 221).

206

207

208

207. Sailing on the Nile (second half of the sixth century AD) Haditha (Lydda district). Length 2.50 m. mosaic
A river-scene is shown, with a schematic representation of a city and the Greek inscription *'Egyptos'* identifying the river as the Nile, with all the pleasures of abundant water: fishes, ducks, lotusflowers, and a sailing-boat carrying wine-jars. The inscriptions appearing in adjacent parts of the floor indicate that this mosaic belonged to a Christian chapel. Here again it seems that both Christians and their Jewish contemporaries (see pl. 235) sometimes preferred worldly and light-hearted representations on the floors of buildings, otherwise dedicated to grave and divine matters.

208. Part of the Main Exhibition Hall
A Roman stone-anchor, as used by local merchantmen, is in the foreground; the model of a second to third-century AD Sidonian merchantman is in the showcase at the back; to its right is a model of a second-century Roman coastguard ship. In the large showcase in the background are graffiti from Jewish tombs showing ships and maritime subjects on coins, the enlargement being a coin of the Hasmonaean King, Alexander Jannaeus (103–76 BC).

used in different periods, and much valuable material has been assembled to document the part played by Jews, both in antiquity and in modern times, on the high seas. A special section is dedicated to underwater archaeology. A fine library and a cartographic collection with its own study-room cater for the interested visitor and for students. **The Af-Al-Pi-Chen** ('None-the-less'), an immigrant ship used in 1947 to bring some of the remnants of Europe's Jewry through the British Navy's blockade to Israel's shores, has been set up nearby, forming a museum administered by the army authorities. Valuable documents and objects of the period are shown in the hull.

The Museum of Japanese Art, housed in a Japanese-style hall, exhibits in rotation its fine collection of paintings and prints. This system, well suited to both the spirit and the material of Japanese art, and the splendid location of the museum—on one of the main streets of central Carmel—make this a popular museum.

The 'Dagon' Grain Museum: the 'Dagon' Grain Silos, situated at the junction of harbour and railway station, turned their entrance lobby and part of their second floor into a museum in 1955.

Its theme is the story of grain-growing, grain storage, milling and baking in Israel, a country forming part of the ancient 'fertile crescent', stretching from Mesopotamia to Egypt, the first to know the cultivation of grain. Its exhibition ranges from botany to archaeology and Jewish ethnography, as far as is relevant to its main subject, much of its collection being the gift of Dagon's director, Dr R. Hecht.

The Golnizki Museum, privately owned and housed on a much more modest scale, was opened to the public in 1968, exhibiting an astonishingly rich collection of Jewish ethnography.

The Museal Youth Services are centrally provided by the Municipality's Education Department which, with its specialized group of teachers, reaches into the museums of the city.

210. Lyre on a Coin (AD 132–135) Israel. Diam. 0.02 m. silver
The obverse carries the first name of Bar Kokhba—Shim'on—in a wreath. The reverse, shown here, has the representation of a three-stringed lyre with a bucket-shaped body. This and other musical instruments appearing on Bar Kokhba's coins were used in the Temple Service. The allusion to the Temple and the Hebrew inscription, 'For the Freedom of Jerusalem', clearly state the reason for the Jews' struggle against Rome.

209. Tambourine Player (end ninth century BC) Shikmona. Height 0.24 m. terracotta
This Phoenician figurine in the Museum of Ancient Art comes from the extensive excavations on the ancient site of Shikmona, at the foot of Mount Carmel's promontory, at the entrance to Haifa. These excavations have to date yielded many finds ranging from the tenth century BC to the sixth century AD. The significance of these figurines is not really certain; some were found in tombs, where they may have been left to give pleasure to the deceased, as they had to the living.

211. Lyre Player (3150–2850 BC) Megiddo. Height 0.15 m. stone
This graffito is one of a group scratched onto the pavement stones in a very early layer of the ancient mount of Megiddo (see pl. 266–7). The group includes pictures of the hunt, a dancer and this musician; it may have had some connection with a magic ceremony intended to help in the hunt. The graffito shows a musician, probably a man, playing on an eight- or nine-string lyre. It must be considered one of the earliest representations of a stringed instrument. (For an even earlier representation of a ceremonial dance, see pl. II/279.)

211

212

212. Af-Al-Pi-Chen

This ship, whose Hebrew name translated literally means 'None-the-less,' was one of the small, unsuitable and often scarcely seaworthy ships, which (like the famous *Exodus*) after World War II brought the remnants of Europe's Jews out of the deathcamps and partisans' hideouts to the shores of Israel, in what was at that time known as 'illegal immigration'. In 1947, the small craft had four hundred and thirty-four refugees on board, when it was captured off Gaza by the British Navy, brought into Haifa harbour, and its Jews deported to Cyprus. Eventually, both the refugees and the ship reached Israel's shores. Part of the ship has been reconstructed to its 1947 condition.

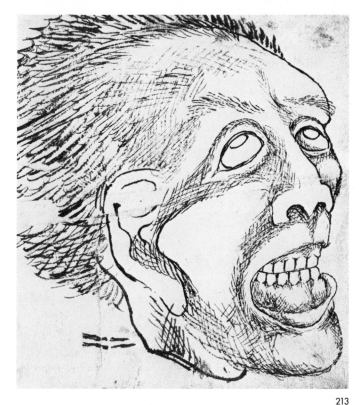

213

213. Hokusai (1760–1849, Japan) *Spectral Face*. 0.16 × 0.15
m. ink on paper
Restless, constantly exploring, Hokusai was for a time
influenced by Western artistic concepts, though his work
remained fundamentally Japanese. He strove to show the
inter-relation between landscape, animal and man, to which
he dedicated a great part of his work. This is just one example
of Hokusai's many sketches of grotesque heads.

214

214. Maruyama Okyo (1733–95, Japan) *Two Monkeys*
(dated Spring 1778). 1 × 0.32 m. ink and colour on silk
The expression of the monkey at rest is realistically rendered
by the brushwork of the painter, who was forty-five years of
age at the time of this fine study, and at the height of his
powers of observation. Western influence in the use of
perspective and shade can be seen.

215. *Colour plate XXXIX.* **Ando Kaigetsudo** (*c.*1671–1743,
Japan) *Courtesan* (1710–15). 0.87 × 0.40 m. colour on silk.
This Kakemono represents a courtesan from the entertainment quarter of Edo, as Tokyo was named in those days. The
stiff folds of the richly decorated garments contrast sharply
with the pale face and black hair of the lady. Erotic entertainment as a strictly organized ritual has been beautifully
expressed by the artist, who still manages to give us an
individual's portrait.

'DAGON' GRAIN MUSEUM

216. Grain as Motif on Coins and Gems

Wheat and barley, both single ears and sheaves symbolizing abundance, appear on many ancient coins and gems of the Mediterranean region. Only a small part of the museum's fine exhibition of this subject is shown here. *Top row, left to right:*

Tetradrachm of Alexander the Great (end of fourth century BC). Diam. 0.024 m. silver
The enthroned Zeus has in front of him an ear of barley.

Roman Sestertius (AD 80). Diam. 0.03 m. bronze
Annona, personification of the yearly corn supply, holds the horn of plenty in one hand and in the other a statuette of Aequitas, personification of equity. At her back is the stern of a ship, signifying the import of corn, while at her feet stands a modius—a large measuring-vessel—filled with a sheaf of wheat.
Middle Row:

Gem-stone (fourth century AD). Diam. 0.02 × 0.015 m.
Fortuna holds an ear of wheat in her right hand and the horn of plenty in her left; a steering oar is at her back and a sheaf of wheat at her feet, perhaps in a modius.

City-Coin of Gaza (AD 5–6). Diam. 0.02 m. bronze
The City-goddess is holding a laurel branch and two ears of barley. The Greek inscription indicates the date.

City-Coin of Caesarea (AD 8–9). Diam. 0.016 m. bronze
An ear of barley is displayed, a Greek inscription names the city.
Bottom Row

Seal-stone (second century AD) Diam. 0.013 × 0.01 m.
Scales lie across the modius, from which issue two ears of barley.

Coin of King Agrippa I of Judea (AD 42–43). Diam. 0.016 m. bronze
Three ears of barley are flanked by the date in Greek. This design was adopted by the State of Israel for one of its coins and by the Dagon Silos as their emblem.

City-Coin of Philadelphia (AD 79). Diam. 0.016 m. bronze
It shows five ears of wheat and the date in Greek.

217. The Baker (third century BC)
Egypt. Height 0.10 m. terracotta
A realistic little figurine, characteristic of Alexandrine art, representing a baker, probably an African, kneading and forming his pyramid-shaped loaves of bread. Such figurines, catching the expression, the movement, and the mood of humble folk at work and play, are characteristic of Hellenistic art, of which this is an excellent example.

218. Entrance Hall
The entrance-hall of the country's central grain silos has been converted into a museum dedicated to the first of the three main products of ancient Israel: corn, wine and oil, mentioned time and again in this order in the Bible. The theme is indicated in the background photographs. The showcases display a rich collection of antiquities and objects of local and Jewish ethnography, connected with the origin of grain, its cultivation, storage, milling, baking, and consumption, as well as its cultural and religious aspects.

217

218

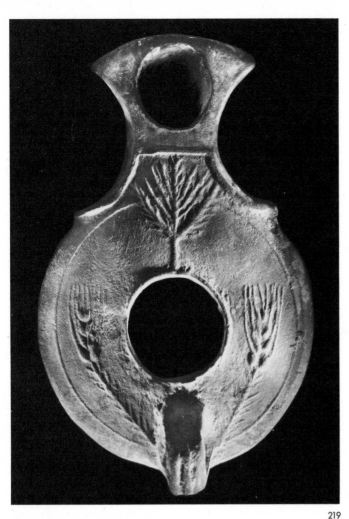

219. Oil Lamp (AD 70–135) Judaean Mountains. Length 0.10 m. pottery

For its decoration this lamp has two ears of barley and a stylized tree, perhaps intended to represent a pine sapling. The decoration on lamps of this type includes motifs connected with a farmer's daily chores, with Jewish feasts and with the seven species with which the Land of Israel was blessed: 'a land of wheat and barley, and vines, and fig trees, and pomegranates, a land of olive oil and honey' (Deut. 8:8).

These lamps are found exclusively in the region and period indicated here, and should be seen as Judaean folk-art of the period between the two wars against Rome.

220. Bread Tray (early twentieth century) Germany. Length (with handles) 0.37 m. porcelain

Such trays were used to hold the two braided loaves of white wheat bread (Hallah) gracing the Shabbat table. The inscription, in Hebrew letters, but in German-Jewish language, reads: 'Gut Shabbos' (Good Shabbat). For the practising Jew every meal starts with the benediction over the bread, dipped into salt. The two Shabbat-loaves—in memory of Shabbat's double portion of manna in the desert (Ex. 16:5)—are covered (see pl. 78) symbolically in order to preserve them from shame at relinquishing their normal precedence to the wine, over which the first benediction is spoken on Shabbat and feast eves, together with the benediction for the day's occasion.

219

220

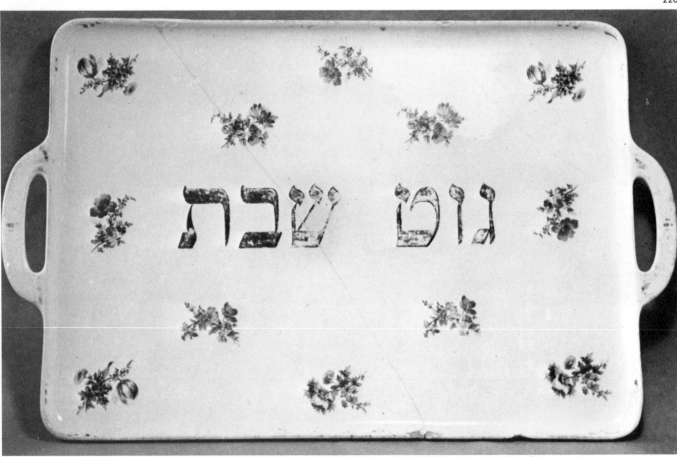

MUSEUMS OF OTHER CITIES

The smaller cities mainly show local archaeology and history in their museums though some also feature modern art. The **Nahariyyah Museum** displays a fine archaeological exhibition, ranging from Prehistory to the Byzantine period, including finds from a seventeenth-century BC 'high place', and fine glass from tombs of the third century AD. **Acre** combines an archaeological exhibition with an ethnographical one, dedicated to Arab and Druze folklore, both shown in the setting of an ancient Turkish bath; all this connected with very fine Crusader architecture, to be visited nearby. At **Tiberias**, in a small museum near the shores of Lake Kinneret (Sea of Galilee), interesting finds from ancient synagogues and tombs are exhibited. Not far away, near the city's hot springs, both the installation of the springs, dating from Roman times and an exceptionally

NAHARIYYAH

221. Seven-cup Offering Vessel (1750–1550 BC) Nahariyyah. Height 0.065 m. diam. 0.10 m. pottery
One of the many pottery vessels, a bowl containing seven small cups, found on and near the high-place of Nahariyyah. The cups may have held some liquid offerings—food, or precious oils and perfumes. Seven-wick pottery lamps found with them suggest that the number had a symbolical significance at this time, in this part of the world.

222. The Nahariyyah Goddess
(1750–1550 BC) Nahariyyah. Height
0.22 m. stone
The mould was discovered between a
temple and a high-place excavated
near Nahariyyah's sea-shore; the cast
shown at its side is modern. The horned
goddess presumably represents Asherat-
Yam (Asherah-of-the-Sea), the Great
Goddess of the Canaanite city of
Ugarit and of the sea-faring Canaanite
traders and artisans. Finding the mould
in this religious centre strongly suggests
the local manufacturing of holy images
for the benefit of the worshippers, who
left evidence of their sacrificial meals in
the many fireplaces, cooking-pots and
sheep-bones found between the temple
and the high-place, and by their
offering-vessels upon the latter.

223. Anthropomorphic Sarcophagus (fifth century BC) Regbah. Height 1.05 m. stone

This upper half of a coffin's lid, found south of Nahariyyah, reminds one slightly of the majestic stone-sarcophagi of Sidon. Here, however, the Phoenician style, using Egyptian elements, was copied by a local artisan lacking all knowledge of the first prototype: the long and narrow beard of the Egyptian mummy has become a short stump under the chin, while the two folds of the Egyptian head-dress have here become two meaningless bars, unconnected with the head.

beautiful mosaic floor of a fourth-century AD synagogue can be seen. **Beth Shean** shows in its city museum rich finds from local Roman tombs, synagogues and churches, while its ancient treasures—a magnificent Roman theatre and a Byzantine monastery's mosaic floors—can be seen in situ.

The cities of the coastal plain around Tel Aviv—**Herzliya, Ramat-Gan** and **Bat Yam**—cater to their public with exhibitions of modern art, whenever possible bringing exhibitions into their halls. Bat Yam also has a museum dedicated to the work of a single artist of Russian-Jewish origin, Issachar Ryback. **Azor**, east of Tel Aviv, has its own small site-museum, displaying local finds, while **Petah Tiqva** has a collection of modern Israeli art and an interesting exhibition showing its local history from the time of its foundation, almost a century ago.

175

Beersheba's Municipal Museum includes a small art collection, some ethnography and modern history, but consists mainly of an excellent exhibition of the city and district's ancient history and archaeology. To these collections are now added some of the finds from excavations of Beersheba's ancient site, covering the twelfth century BC—the period of Israel's Judges—to the Persian era; it has a Roman fortress of the first to second century AD at the top level. A street containing the remains of houses of the ancient city is now being preserved.

Both **Dimona** and **Elath** in the South have the beginnings of small municipal museums of art. The latter has also a small but interesting museum dedicated to marine life, the only one concentrating on the Red Sea.

ACRE

224. Druze and Arab Folklore

The setting for this display is the main hall of Acre's old Turkish Bath, built in 1785 by Jazzar Pasha, as was the beautiful Mosque nearby. The ornamentation of the floor-tiles and the central fountain is characteristic of that period. Among the groups of models the one in the centre background shows a Druze house interior where the men are having coffee, while in the room nearby, strictly separated from the men, the woman of the house attends to her baby. To the right we see a street scene in Acre: here is a seller of brass and copper vessels, identified by his *kaffiya* as a villager, while a citizen sits in the foreground, sipping his coffee in a small coffee-house.

225

225. Refectory of the Knights of St John (mid-twelfth century AD) Acre
This majestic hall, with its cross-ribbed vaults resting on three heavy columns, is an early example of the transition from the Romanesque to the Gothic style. It was part of the Hospice of the Knights of St John, being originally connected with the living quarters and the hospital of the Order by a subterranean passage, entered near the column in the foreground.

TIBERIAS

226. Menorah Relief (third to fourth century AD) Tiberias region. Height 0.40 m. basalt
This Menorah, flanked by a rather clumsily indicated ram's horn, palm branch and citrus fruit, must have once adorned one of the many small synagogues that served the Jewish farmers in the villages around Lake Kinneret.

227. Tomb Door (third to fourth century AD) Tiberias. Height 1.30 m. basalt
This door, which once closed one of the many Jewish rock-tombs of the region, is characteristic of Roman stone doors, which imitate panelled wood-work strengthened by metal-strips, and heavy nails indicating the knocker, the pull-ring and two keys. The material is the local black basalt, rough and very strong. (See also pl. 202.)

228

228. Hammath-Tiberias Synagogue Floor, detail (fourth century AD). Length of outer frame 2 m. mosaic

Detail of the floor of a large synagogue, discovered near the hot springs of Tiberias, at a site called in antiquity Hamm'tha ('Hot Springs'). In the centre of the floor is a representation of Helios surrounded by the signs of the Zodiac with dedicatory inscriptions below. The section shown here lies before the holy ark. This ark is depicted in the centre of the panel, flanked by two seven-branched menorahs, their flames strangely turned each to its centre, according to a belief that the Spirit of the Lord rested upon the flames. Each menorah has on one side a ram's horn and an incense-shovel and on the other the palm branch and the citrus fruit, thus hinting at the season of the Jewish high holidays: New Year, when the ram's horn is sounded; Day of Atonement, the only day of the year on which the High-Priest goes into the Holy of Holies of Jerusalem's Temple, to atone for himself, his house and all of Israel, offering incense; and the Feast of the Tabernacles, when the Congregation of Israel walks in procession in the synagogues carrying the branches and fruits of the Land of Israel. The choice of the attributes of this feast in preference to those of the other important feasts may have been caused not only by its calendarial proximity to the New Year, but also because it was considered the season when the amount of the coming winter's rainfall was decided upon by the Lord; a crucial factor in a country with a poor water-supply. Even nowadays Lake Kinneret (The Sea of Galilee), recedes after a winter of little rain.

229

230

BETH SHEAN

229. Roman Theatre (early third century AD) Beth Shean
Excavated in 1962, this is the largest surviving Roman theatre in the country, seating some eight thousand people. It was built under Septimius Severus and was used until AD 450. In the right background rises the ancient site of Beth Shean, with its eighteen occupation levels, ranging from 3500 BC to about AD 1200. Finds from both sites are exhibited in the Municipal Museum, as well as in the central museums of Jerusalem.

230. Sarcophagus Lid (first half of the third century AD) Beth Shean. Length 2.45 m. limestone
An important citizen of Scythopolis, as Beth Shean was then called, is reclining, clad in tunic and toga, the *mappa*, his ceremonial kerchief, in his hand. The *mappa* was used by officials to announce the beginning of games at the hippodrome or circus.

231. Censer and Menorah (end sixth century AD) Beth Shean. Heights 0.18 and 0.09 m. bronze
Both objects come from the destruction-layer of a synagogue, which stood until about AD 620, and can be thus dated accordingly. The Menorah originally formed the handle of an oil lamp. Some of these lamps, as with other objects of the period, proclaimed the faith of their owner only by the addition of either Menorah or Cross. Censers also were used at that time by both Jews and Christians; by the former in continuation of a Roman custom at the end of a festive meal when burning spices were brought in, to give pleasure to the participants. This custom is, however, different from the use of pleasant-smelling spices at the end of the Shabbat ceremonies—a Jewish religious custom which dates back to the first century AD and is still being practised (see pl. 114). It seems likely that this censer was used at the end of a festive meal in the synagogue compound, rather than in a religious ceremony, as is customary with Christians, who since the fourth century AD have been using incense.

233

232. *Colour plate XLVI.* **Negro Leading a Giraffe** (*c.* AD 567) Beth Shean. Diam. 0.60 m. mosaic

Detail of a mosaic-floor from the Monastery of the Lady Mary at Beth Shean. The whole floor depicts rural, hunting and exotic scenes, each one inscribed inside a circle formed by the scrolls of a large grape-vine emerging from an amphora. Such floors have recurring motifs, appearing both in this and in other countries at that period. It is evident that they were executed by artisans who worked with pattern-books, from which the prospective customer made his choice. The floor is kept on the site of its discovery. (See also pl. 244.)

BAT YAM

233. Issachar Rybak (1897–1935, Russia) *The Artist's Wife* (1931). 0.46 × 0.38 m. oil on canvas.

Born in a small Ukrainian village, Rybak first studied art in Russia and then, from 1921, in Berlin. The cubism of his early work soon gave place to a lyric realism, though sombre hues dominate. In 1926 he went to Paris, where he lived until his sudden death at the age of thirty-seven. His work included a number of ceramic figurines, imbued with a warm-hearted irony. His work finally achieved a serenity and tenderness rare in modern art and very well represented in this painting of his young wife.

234

235

BEERSHEBA

234. Kitchen Ware (eighth century BC)
Beersheba. Pottery
From layers belonging to the time of the
Judaean kingdom, the ancient site of
Beersheba has yielded, besides the remains of a local temple, a whole street
of eighth- to seventh-century BC houses.
Domestic pottery found there can be
seen in the museum. Here are wares
from the houses of practically every
Judaean citizen or farmer of that period:
the hole-mouth jar for water or oil, top
right, with the small dipper-juglet in the
foreground; the wine decanter far right;
left, a heavy cooking-pot and small
cooking-jar; in the centre a food dish,
while an oil-lamp (diameter 0.28 m.) is
in the foreground.

235. The Leontis Mosaic (mid-fifth
century AD) Beth Shean. Height of
detail 0.80 m.
Section of a large mosaic floor in a room
which is part of a complex comprising
a synagogue and other congregational
buildings. The floor includes representations of Odysseus's adventure with the
Sirens (Od. 12:178 ff.) and a Nilotic
scene, its lower part showing a boat
loaded with wine-jars. The Nile emerges
from the jar beneath the arm of the
river-god, shown here. He is resting on a
crocodile, a reed in his left hand, a
waterbird in his right. The schematic
building to his right is identified by its
Greek inscription as Alexandria; under
it a bullock is attacked by some fero-
cious animal. A Greek inscription in the
centre-panel of the floor identifies its

donor as Kyrios Leontis Kloubas, obviously a wealthy and important member of the community. It is interesting to
compare this floor, full of exotic and
entertaining pictures in a building
dedicated to Jewish religious purposes,
with the very similar one in the Christian Chapel at Haditha (pl. 207).

236. *Colour plate XLVII.* **Coiled Snake**
(sixth century AD) Beersheba. Diam.
0.60 m. detail of a mosaic floor's border
The snake is one of a row of exotic
animals, each with its own medallion
(see also pl. 232), which surround a
fairly plain floor of a room in a farm
complex of the Byzantine period—a
time of prosperity for the country at
large.

237. Beth Ussishkin
This museum was built at Kibbutz Dan by the architect Leopold Krakauer (1890–1954). It combines functionalism and a genuine feeling for landscape and local material. (For Krakauer's graphic work see pl. 252.)

DISTRICT MUSEUMS

In some of the kibbutzes of Israel, often from the earliest days of their foundation, a member would start to collect the chance finds brought up by cultivator or plough, or plants and animals encountered in his settlement's immediate surroundings. He would perhaps become interested in a site abandoned a thousand—or a hundred—years before, or in out-dated agricultural and domestic implements discarded by his Arab or Druze neighbours. Such items were at first collected into some old orange-box and slightly shame-facedly hidden under the bed. Eventually, however, the kibbutz would give its enthusiastic member the freedom of some unused wooden shed so that he could keep his finds, just as might be done for a member who painted or sculpted. In many cases, some items from these collections would eventually be displayed in showcases in the reading-room of the kibbutz, either to be proudly shown to visitors or else to be forgotten, should the initiator have died or left. In other cases, however, where collectors were more persistent, or luckier in raising district interest, collections have grown into real museums. Their upkeep is assured either by the kibbutz where they are located, by the District Council, or by the State. The museum curators are sometimes the original collector and they often receive the necessary academic education in their special subject, and also instruction in running a museum.

The museums so evolved are by their very nature dedicated to the study and display of plant- and wild-life, ethnography, archaeology or history of the district. The emphasis will often depend on the

238

238. Oak Grove, Diorama
A robin, a tit and a scops owl clutching a field-mouse, are seen in the undergrowth of an oak grove, characteristic of the Huleh region, a district only recently drained. It still retains two ancient groves, protected as national parks: the Dan Grove, one of the sources of the Jordan, and the Tal Grove on the banks of the Dan stream, another source of the Jordan. Both contain trees over a thousand years old, though the grove as an entity must be much older. Such groves were held in veneration since ancient times: single oaks and groves are mentioned in the Bible as sanctified seats of judgment, prophecy and royal assembly (Gen. 12:6; Jud. 2:1, 9:6, 9:37). The different peoples settling near them adapted their religious concepts to the local tradition. Some of these trees and groves were venerated until modern times and thus survived.

curator's own inclinations. Most of these museums, as well as many of the city museums, get State subsidies, according to their usefulness to the public at large and to the schools of the district. They furthermore receive State assistance in all matters pertaining to museology as well as in the centralized registration of antiquities found in their collections, their defining, preservation and proper display.

Starting in the north of the country, the first district museum encountered is **Beth Ussishkin** at Kibbutz Dan, founded in 1955 and housed in a beautifully situated and perfectly balanced building, planned by the late architect, Leo Krakauer. This museum contains a professionally organized display of the plant- and wild-life of the Huleh region, one of Israel's main swamps before drainage. This display is complemented by the nature-reserves near by: the sources of the Jordan at Tel Dan to the north, a small part of the swamps which have been preserved to the south. The exhibitions of natural history at the museum have recently been augmented by material from the Golan Heights. The museum includes both systematic displays and dioramas, showing wild-life and plants of the region at different times of the year. There is also a small display of antiquities here, including very important Roman items, as well as finds from the site at Dan. **Ma'yan Barukh**, nearby, concentrates on the prehistory of the region which has here been systematically assembled. It is very comprehensively displayed though still housed in wooden huts. A permanent building is under construction.

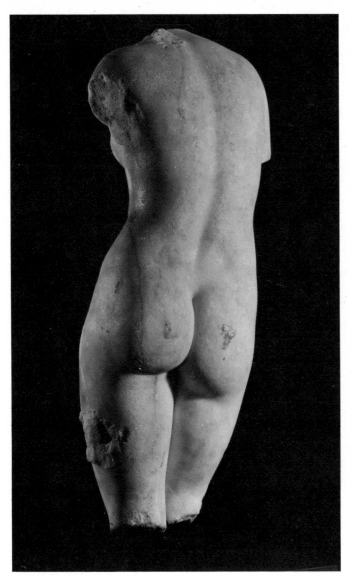

239

240

239. The Dan Venus (first century BC) Dan region. Present height 0.66 m. marble

This very fine statue was discovered in the fields of Kibbutz Dan. Even though it lacks head, feet, and arms which once shielded the breasts and lower body, it can be recognized as a Roman copy of the famous *Venus Pudica*, the Venus of Modesty. This replica is nearest in style to the famous Aphrodite Medici, which is a first-century BC copy after an original of the Praxitelean school.

240. Boar under Cypress (sixth century AD) Hanitha. Height 2.80 m. mosaic

The Museum at Kibbutz Hanitha occupies an ancient Arab building, which in turn took over the remains of a Byzantine church of the sixth century; some of the latter's walls still stand. Excavations on the site revealed parts of the church, including the floor of the narthex (7 × 13 m.) which carries remains of a figurative mosaic depicting what is probably part of a hunting scene: a boar standing near a stylized cypress.

EN HAROD REGIONAL MUSEUM

241. Beth Sturman (1941)
The way leading up to this museum is bordered with Roman milestones gathered from the fields of the region, which nowadays cover the ancient Roman roads. But wherever a modern road follows the ancient one, and such milestones have been found along it, they have been set up and kept at their original site.

Hanitha, on the north-western border of the country, has its own museum, part of which is housed in a sixth-century church; mosaics from the latter are displayed on the site. Here too is an exhibition of the history of the Hanitha Kibbutz, which was started during the 1938 riots, when a stockade and watch-tower were erected there overnight, to withstand attack. At Deganyah, the first kibbutz to be founded in Israel in 1907, the members and settlers from the vicinity established **Beth Gordon** in 1935, an Agricultural and Nature Study Institute, which now adds an exhibition of archaeological finds to its rich collection of animals, plants, and inorganic material of the central Jordan valley. It also administers an observatory and a large library.

Beth Sturman, founded in 1941 at the large En Harod Kibbutz, is now a comprehensive district museum, including finds from the Beth Shean valley in one direction to the slopes of Mount Gilboa in the other. Roman milestones greet the visitor at the museum's entrance, collected from fields covering former imperial roads. Its archaeological finds include Canaanite and Egyptian statuettes, synagogue lintels and church mosaics; its historic display tells the story of the drainage of this valley in 1921, when it was a malaria-infested swamp unfit for human occupation, describes the irrigation of the fields, and shows the agricultural and economic problems of the district. A good zoological collection, together with archives and study-rooms, completes the exhibition.

Mishkan le-Omanut, En Harod's large Museum of Art, was founded in 1938 by a local artist named Haim Atar; it moved into its present spacious premises, designed by Samuel Bikels, in 1948; even these are at present too small to display its representative collection of Jewish plastic arts, mainly painting and graphics. It starts with the genre painters of the nineteenth century in Germany, Poland and Russia and includes Jewish painters of the Ecole de Paris as well as those of the Realist and Impressionist schools of Western Europe and

to p.190

242

242. Group of Tomb Busts (third to fourth century AD) Beth Shean Valley. Average height 0.50 m. stone
Such busts were put into niches in the ante-room of family tombs, in accordance with Roman practice. Characteristic of the local art of the period, some of them carry the name of the deceased in Greek letters. The tomb-stele in the background representing a rider and his attendant is worthy of attention; it is late Hellenistic or early Roman.

243. Figurine of Bastet (thirteenth century BC) Beth Shean. 0.11 m. bronze
Cats were deified in Egypt from early periods, and already domesticated there in the second millennium BC; it is possible that they came from that country via Greece into Europe. Egyptians identified a former lioness-goddess with Bastet, though in her manifestations as cat she represented the friendly nature of the felines, while as Sekhmet, the lioness-headed goddess, she expressed their ferocity. This figurine must have originally carried, as did most of its kind, a basket and a sistrum, symbols of happiness, music, and feasting; but she also holds the lioness-mask of Sekhmet, lest we forget her second nature.

244

243

244. Church Floor (fifth century AD) Sedeh Nahum, Beth Shean Valley. Mosaic.

This is part of the broad frame of a floor, measuring originally 11.80 × 6.20 m., belonging to a monastery's church in this region, most prosperous in Byzantine times. The fragment shown includes various animals and birds in the circles of the vine branches; in the upper centre is a vintager. Near him, a fox is stalking some geese, who seem blissfully unaware of the imminent danger. Floors of this period found in different parts of this and the neighbouring countries have many motifs in common; it is clear that they were made by itinerant artisans who showed their pattern-books to prospective customers. It is gratifying to see that our forebears sometimes showed their sense of humour by choosing such scenes for the floors of their houses of prayer, which were decorated with solemn representations on walls and ceiling. It is also amusing to see how this mosaic was subsequently repaired by much less skilful artisans, who put upon the graceful body of the gazelle at the lower left a muzzle, looking rather like a pig's snout.

Russia. American Neo-Realism is also well represented. This museum also succeeded in rescuing from oblivion the work of Jewish painters who were exterminated by the Nazis all over Europe. A special gallery is dedicated to Israeli art from its beginnings some fifty years ago to the present day. All these collections are being enlarged.

The cultural background of these collections is re-created in a section dedicated to Jewish Folk Art from the fifteenth century to the present in all parts of the Diaspora. Here one has the unique experience of seeing the Jewish approach to the plastic arts in different countries and at different times. The impression one receives has been well summed up by Martin Buber, speaking about Jewish creative artists in a paper written in 1902 which is almost prophetic: they 'may . . . introduce new and fructifying elements into art; particularly on the eve of a period whose nature, it appears, is to dissolve all substance into its component relations and transform them into spiritual values'.

Ohel Sarah, near Tel Adashim, on the road from Afulah to Nazareth, was founded by the Jezreel County Council as a district museum, which in 1970 added an exhibition of archaeological finds

MISHKAN LE-OMANUT

245. Isidor Kaufmann (1853–1921, Romania) *Synagogue Interior*. 1.12 × 0.93 m. oil on canvas
Kaufmann was one of the first Jewish genre-painters of the nineteenth century to describe the life of the Hasidic Jews of Poland and Hungary. In his pictures, as in the Hasidic folk-tales, the everyday life of the simple Jew is depicted in detailed naturalism, enclosing the hidden light of mystical experience.

246

247

248

246. Marc Chagall (born 1887, Russia) *The Wandering Musician* (1923). 0.281 × 0.203 m. woodcut
In this rare and early print Chagall's wandering Jew does not yet float over Vitebsk's roof-tops. His pack on his back and his fiddle at his side, he walks alone, delineated with love and a delicate humour. (See also pl. XXI/144.)

247. Max Fabian (1873–1926, Germany) *Refugees* (1902). 1.58 × 1.12 m. oil on canvas.
This painter of the life of Berlin's poor expressed here his feelings on encountering Jewish refugees from the Russian pogroms at the beginning of this century.

248. Joseph Budko (1888–1920, Poland) *Market Place in Town* (1930). 1 × 0.90 m. oil on canvas
Budko should be counted amongst Berlin's graphic artists of the nineteen-twenties; yet his main output consisted of drawings, etchings, and woodcuts in which he caught the life of Poland's Jews. In this painting Budko succeeds in expressing in sombre tones the sadness and hopelessness of life in the Jewish townlet—the 'Shtetl'.

249

249. Anna Ticho (born 1894, Moravia) *Trees in the Evening*
(1962). 0.71 × 0.50 m. chalk on paper
Since coming from Moravia in 1912, Anna Ticho has dedicated her work to the rendering of Jerusalem's hills and rocks,
trees and houses, with the love and precision of the masters of
bygone ages. Hers is the quiet song of devotion, of love and
awe towards the landscape of the Lord's prophets.

250. Yehiel Shemi (born 1921, Poland) *Mother and Child*
(1952). Height 1.97 m. wood
A Member of Kibbutz Kabri and of the New Horizons group
of artists, Shemi has always aimed at new means of expression;
these have lately brought him to the creation of neo-figurative
monuments in concrete and iron, set up in different parts of
the country. In the wooden figure of the mother and child,
Shemi wished to express his feelings towards the holocaust
which destroyed Europe's Jews.

250

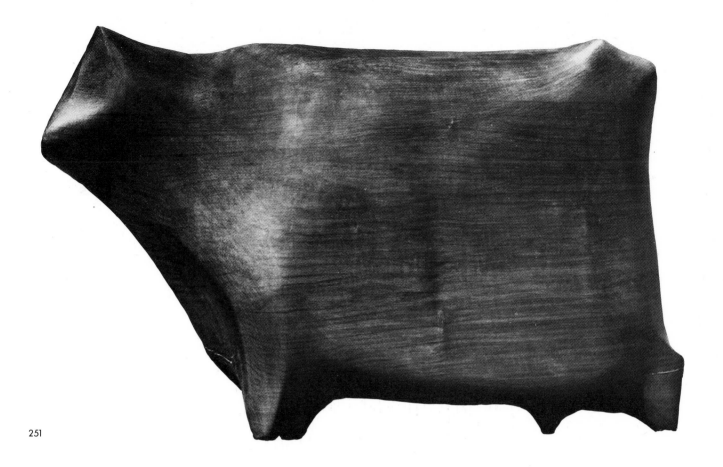

251

251. Aharon Bezalel (born 1925, Afghanistan) *Cow* (1962). Height 0.29 m. wood

Bezalel came to this country in his youth, but his work combines elements of Near-Eastern antiquities with Western techniques, acquired from his teachers in Jerusalem. His feeling for form is well expressed in the rendering of the cow's heavy, yet soft body.

to a collection of works by local artists. The items shown correspond to the surrounding landscape, for here is a rare and beautiful instance when the sites where the finds were discovered can be seen through the museum's large windows: finds from prehistoric caves on Mount Hakephitza and vessels from the fields near the Kishon river, where the Prophetess Deborah and her field-commander Barak defeated the iron chariots of the Canaanite king of Hazor (Judges 4–5). A unique exhibit is a jar burial made between the twelfth and eleventh centuries BC—perhaps that of a Hittite.

Midreshet Ruppin, at Kefar Monash near Netanyah, houses a museum established in 1958 by the Emek Hefer District Council. This museum includes a very good natural history section, displaying the wild life along the central coast of Israel, concentrating especially on birds, both local and migratory. It also has an archaeological section, set up by the Antiquities Department's District archaeologist.

The Shephelah District Museum at Kefar Menahem was established in its premises in 1963. It comprises an archaeological exhibition and the beginnings of an art collection, mainly by local artists. Its main activities are educational and are second only to those of the Israel Museum's Youth Wing. It was characteristic of this museum's approach that its first permanent building to be erected in 1973 was dedicated to these activities.

In this connection it should be emphasized that all the above-mentioned district museums serve both their local schools and also

252

252. Leopold Krakauer (1890–1954, Austria) *Hills near Jerusalem* (1952). 0.69 × 0.56 m. chalk on paper

Krakauer, architect and draughtsman, expressed in his buildings as well as in his drawings his deep understanding and love for Israel's landscape. Disciplining his strong emotions, he set buildings into this landscape which were perfectly attuned to their surroundings (see pl. 237) and captured Jerusalem's hills, olive trees and undergrowth in a manner which brings to mind Wordsworth's 'spontaneous overflow of powerful feelings, recollected in tranquility'.

visiting classes from all parts of the country with guided tours, courses in the plastic arts and excursions to ancient sites and the nearby nature reserves. In the latter activity, the Field Schools of the country take special pride. However, **En Gedi**, overlooking the Dead Sea, is the only one of these to have added a small museum of nature reserve specimens and archaeological finds to the intensive study of a given district. The sites there include a mid-fourth-century BC temple, a fifth-century AD synagogue, and a nature reserve which brings gazelles from the desert right to the museum's lawn.

253. Torah Case (1847) North Africa. Height 0.79 m. silver, *repoussé*
The Torah, the handwritten parchment-scroll of the Five Books of Moses, is encased here in a metal container, opening on a hinge, in the fashion of the Oriental Jews. The case is ornamented with Hispano-Mauresque motifs, still used by Mediterranean Jews over four hundred years after their expulsion from Spain, just as they kept alive the Castilian language in their own Hispano-Jewish language, Ladino.

254. *Colour plate XXIX.* **Shalom Moscovitz of Safed** (born Israel) *Rebekah and Jacob* (1956). 0.48 × 0.32 m. gouache on paper.
'Shalom the Watchmaker', as he is known in Safed, started painting late in life, around 1950. His sole theme is the Bible, set naively in his immediate surroundings: the houses and courtyards of Safed, and the surrounding villages, fields and mountains. Citizens and villagers, Jewish and Arab neighbours, become models for the heroes of biblical stories. Here Rebekah is shown instructing Jacob how to obtain Isaac's blessing—Gen. 27:6–10 being actually quoted in the Hebrew script. Isaac is shown occupied in the most plausible, though completely anachronistic, manner as the orthodox Jewish head of an important family: 'Isaac stands and prays in his Synagogue', as the nearby inscription indicates.

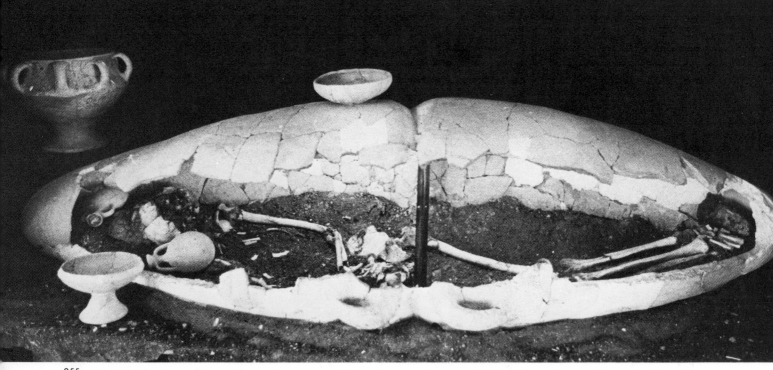

OHEL SARAH

255. Jar Burial (twelfth to eleventh centuries BC) Kefar Yehoshu'a. Length 1.82 m. pottery

Burials of adults in jars were very rare in Israel, though common among Hittites living towards the end of their empire around 1200 BC. Thus one is tempted to view this as the burial of an important Hittite, perhaps one of the king's envoys to the court of Egypt's Pharaoh. If so, he was buried by his faithful servants according to his homeland's custom, albeit using local vessels.

MIDRESHET RUPPIN

256. Detail of Coffin (first half of third century AD) Kafar Vitkin. Height 0.40 m. lead

The photograph shows the narrow side of a lead coffin which belonged to a young man of some thirty-eight years of age, probably a well-to-do farmer, living in the region whose centre was the city of Caesarea. A winged sphinx upon a Doric column brings to mind the famous votive present given by the people of Naxos to the Temple of Delos in the sixth century BC—a representation often depicted at later times on Hellenistic and early Roman tombstones. Here it is encountered for the first time at a much later date, flanked by Apollo and by dolphins. It is doubtful whether the manufacturers of such coffins, using ready-made stamps for this sort of ornamentation, would have cared or even known what the original significance of these figures had been. (See also pl. 54.)

256

LOCAL AND
SITE MUSEUMS

Some of the local and site museums of the country have also developed from local kibbutz collections, four having so far attained museum status: **Sasa** in central Galilee, located in a fine old building, exhibits local finds as well as ethnographic material, illustrating Arab and Druze village life; Kibbutz **Sha'ar Ha-Golan**, between the rivers Jordan and Yarmuk, exhibits in its small museum, formerly a bomb-shelter, some very interesting finds from the second half of the fifth millennium BC, including some unique figurines. A separately-housed collection includes much important ethnographic material of the region. It is hoped that both these collections will be concentrated in one suitable building in the near future.

Nazareth has a small site-museum near the large modern Church of the Annunciation, which shows finds made when the foundations of this church were dug and at some previous excavations at the site. These include pottery from the late Canaanite and Israelite periods, some items from Hellenistic and Herodian times and much material from later Roman, Byzantine and Mediaeval times. Some of the remains of the Byzantine church of the fifth to sixth centuries, its central apse and the Sacred Grotto of the Annunciation, have been left uncovered in the centre of the modern church—a most striking and unusual sight. According to its excavators, the Franciscan Fathers of the Holy Land Custody, the graffiti on the walls of these remains were made by third-century pilgrims; these graffiti are believed to include references to the Marian cult some two hundred years before it was officially accepted by the Council of Ephesus in AD 431.

The most important exhibitions are, however, the five Romanesque capitals, some depicting ancient legends connected with the mission of the Apostles, others with Jesus's visits to Galilee. These capitals seem to have been the work of French artists from Burgundy or Berry, who worked on them until 1187, when Saladin's advance put an end to their enterprise. The capitals were thus never actually used, but were fortunately hidden by pious hands, to come to light seven hundred and twenty years later.

Ma'barot, between Netanyah and Haderah, a kibbutz in the Sharon plain, includes in its small museum a Middle Canaanite tomb-cave, discovered when the modern building was erected, and

to p.209

257

258

PALAMAHIM

257. Beth Miriam

In this general view we see about half of the Kibbutz museum's main exhibition hall, displaying local finds. A large map in the background indicates where fishing-boats of the Kibbutz found ancient pottery in their dragnets. The left background shows the later archaeological sequences here: from the third century BC on the right, to the first century AD, including a Jewish ossuary (*cf.* pl. 41) on the left. The centre of the hall displays a rare thirteenth-century BC cist-tomb, a huge jar of the seventh-to-eighth-centuries AD and a group of fourth-millennium BC ossuaries. The latter are receptacles for secondary burial of the deceased's bones; some are of baked clay and house-shaped, thus supplying us with information about dwellings of the period. These houses seem to have been built of wooden beams, reed-mats, and other perishable material. Others are simple stone or baked clay receptacles. Similar contemporary ossuaries—both house-shaped and plain—have been found at sites on the coastal plain in the Tel Aviv region, and farther north. It is interesting to see at one glance ossuaries separated in origin by over three thousand years: the pre-historic ones in the foreground, the Jewish one in the showcase behind. There was, however, no continuity of custom; moreover, lacking literary evidence, we know little about the reasons for the rites of re-burial in the former case, being better informed about the latter (see pl. 41).

NAZARETH

258. The Basilica of the Annunciation

The remains of former basilicas have been very effectively included in Nazareth's modern sanctuary of 1969, planned by Giovanni Muzzio and richly adorned by contemporary artists from around the world. The photograph shows part of the left aisle of the basilica, identical in plan with the Crusader church of the twelfth century. To the right are parts of the main apse of the Byzantine church of the fifth to sixth centuries, with some of its columns to the front of the picture. Behind this is the Grotto of the Annunciation, with the seventeenth-century altar belonging to the Franciscan order which has kept this sanctuary ever since. For a scene of the Annunciation on a flask contemporary with the Byzantine church, see pl. 4.

259

259. Crusader Capital (eighth decade of the twelfth century) Nazareth. Height 0.65 m. limestone

This is the largest of the five capitals found in 1908 at the site of the Crusader church which was built in the twelfth century and destroyed in 1263 by Sultan Baybars. The capitals were found where they had been hidden after Saladin's victory at the Horns of Hattin on 4 July 1187 and his later conquest of the country. Their condition leaves no doubt that they were never used. This capital shows Faith, leading a rather hesitant apostle, threatened on both sides by demons. The capitals are very close in style to those found in contemporary churches in the French provinces of Bourgogne and Berry and are thought to be the work of artists who came from there; it may well have been their masters who hid the capitals, hoping for better days.

SHA'AR HA-GOLAN

260. Head of a Figurine (second half of fifth millennium BC) Sha'ar Ha-Golan. Height 0.065 m. clay

This head must have belonged to a figurine similar to that of the Horvat Minha Venus (pl. 10). The close-up gives us a good opportunity to study the head's strong features, achieved by the simple use of small coils and pellets of clay: slanting eyes, prominent nose, small mouth. It was discovered at a site whose culture is called Yarmukian, after the nearby river Yarmuk, flowing into the Jordan . The finds included a workshop of flint implements and some of the earliest pottery made by man.

XXXIV. **Joseph Zaritsky,** *Landscape*. Tel Aviv Museum. (Note 175)

XXXV. **Marcel Janco,** *Turnavitu*, 1968. Tel Aviv Museum. (Note 154)

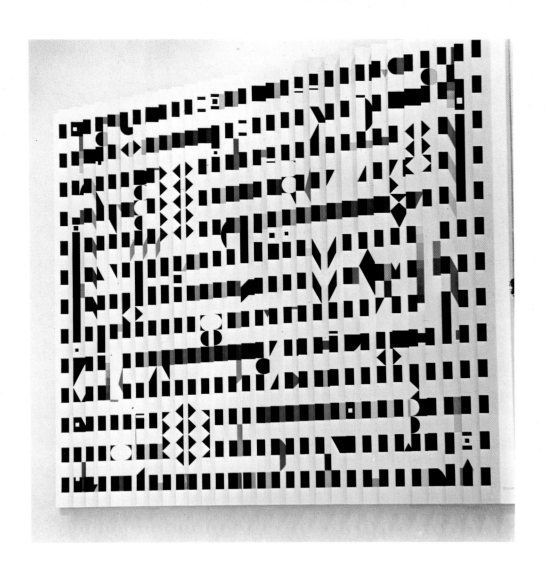

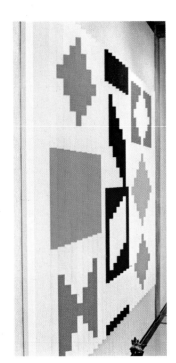

XXXVI. **Yaacov Agam,** *Pace of Time*, 1970. Tel Aviv Museum. (Note 176)

XXXVII. **Nachum Gutman,** *On the Jaffa Road*, 1971. Tel Aviv Museum. (Note 183)

XXXVIII. **The Ennion Jug,** first century AD. Ha'aretz
Museum, Tel Aviv. (Note 189)

XXXIX. **Ando Kaigetsudo,** *Courtesan,* 1710–15.
Museum of Japanese Art, Haifa. (Note 215)

XL. **Marriage-Deed,** 1776. Ha'aretz Museum, Tel Aviv. (Note 197)

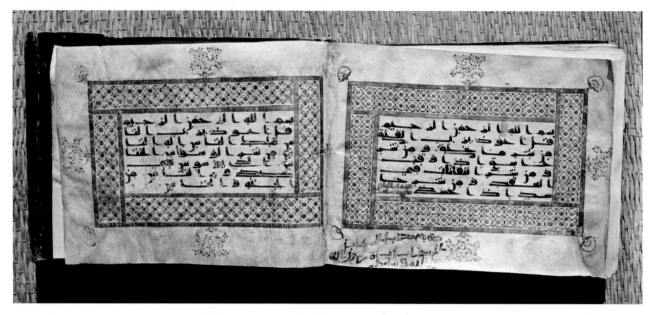

XLI. **Koran,** ninth century. Islamic Museum. (Note 117)

XLII. **The Bird's Head Haggadah,** late fourteenth century. The Israel Museum, Jerusalem. (Note 71)

XLIII. **Illuminated Initial,** late fourteenth century. The Convent of the Flagellation, Jerusalem. (Note 116)

XLIV. **Holy Ark Doors,** seventeenth century. Wolfson Museum, Jerusalem. (Note 118)

XLV. **Ilkhan Casket,** second half of the thirteenth century. Mayer Institute of Islamic Art. (Note 282)

XLVI. **Negro Leading a Giraffe,** Byzantine floor mosaic, *c.* AD 567. Beth Shean Museum. (Note 232)

XLVII. **Coiled Snake,** sixth century AD. Beersheba Museum. (Note 236)

AYELET HA-SHAHAR HAZOR MUSEUM

261. Seated God (thirteenth century BC) Hazor. Height 0.40 m. basalt
This statue was found to the left of a row of steles, most of them lacking any decoration, except for the centre one, which carries two emblems: crescent and disk, and two raised hands. The seated male statue also has a crescent on his breast; his right hand holds a cup. It has been suggested that this sanctuary was dedicated to a moon-god; the raised hands have been interpreted as being connected with this god's consort. while the steles lack of emblems have been interpreted as memorials for the dead.

The Hazor Museum exhibits a replica of this statue; the original is in the Israel Museum, Jerusalem.

reconstructed on the site. This tomb has now had all the finds replaced in the positions in which they were originally unearthed.

Beth Miriam, in Kibbutz Palmahim, situated at the mouth of the Sorek river, exhibits a comprehensive collection of local finds, including house-shaped ossuaries of the fourth millennium BC and a complete reconstruction of a cist-tomb of the fourteenth to thirteenth centuries BC, containing Cypriot imports. The former are of special interest; they include rectangular and beehive-shaped receptacles, into which the bones of primary burials were collected. Their special interest lies in the information they give us of the living quarters of their period. Actually made of perishable materials—wood and rush-mats—they form in this reduced scale the deceased's 'eternal house'. Similar contemporary house-shaped ossuaries have been found in the Tel Aviv region and in the Sharon plain (a large collection of these can be seen at the Israel Museum, Jerusalem). This museum has also a good collection of finds brought up from the depth of the sea by the nets of the fishermen.

Besides its main task of maintaining Israel's many parks, the National Parks Authority administers most of the site museums. These are usually situated near the site; their main purpose is to enhance the visit to the site, to serve as its introduction or its summary. **The Hazor Museum** is actually the only one not located on the site, but somewhat to its north, at Kibbutz Ayelet Ha-Shahar. In the eighteenth century BC the city of Hazor was one of the main

centres of the Middle East. A most important Canaanite centre throughout Egyptian suzerainty, it remained a mighty city, hostile to the Israelites at the period of their conquest. It was rebuilt by Solomon, and remained an Israelite city until its destruction by Tiglath-pileser III in 732 BC. While some of the site's important finds are exhibited in the Israel Museum, many others, including cult-objects, have found their place in the site museum's precincts. To complete the picture, replicas of some of the former items have been included in the presentation.

Beth Shearim, on the road from Nazareth to Haifa, was an important Jewish town from the second to the fourth centuries AD, for a time the seat of the *Sanhedrin*, the Jewish High Court. The small museum—and the many catacombs—contain a large collection of stone sarcophagi, graffiti, inscriptions and architectural detail, witnesses to the culture of this town in its prime. Special interest lies in the abundant contemporary examples of Jewish folk-culture, both in Israel and in the Diaspora, from which the deceased were brought for interment in this hallowed spot. The finds, including sarcophagi decorated with scenes of pagan mythology (among them Leda and the Swan, on exhibition at the Rockefeller Museum) have forced scholars to re-appraise the attitude of Judaism at that time towards figurative art. It seems likely that a certain tolerance towards pagan forms developed, in direct proportion to the disbelief in the pagan mind towards its gods; the majority of people seem to have seen them as no more than decorative patterns of little meaning—a fashion suitable to a certain class of people in the Roman empire.

The site museum, located in one of the catacomb's ancient cisterns, contains one of the world's largest glass blocks, weighing some 8.8 tons, made of a reddish opaque glass and excavated from under the tank in which it was originally made—and where it still remains. It can be dated by pottery sherds to a period between the fourth and sixth centuries AD. Clearly, the glass was melted on the spot at a very high temperature, to remain as a cast slab, though its purpose is less clear. But it is possible that it was merely intended as a production of glass-mass, to be broken up eventually for sale to glass-makers as raw material; why it was never used remains a riddle.

Megiddo, at the northern end of the narrow pass cutting through the Carmel range, has held, since antiquity, the key to the main gate of 'the Way to the Sea' (Isa. 9:1), which led from Egypt to Damascus and beyond; in fact, it is the gateway of the main road on the land-bridge between Africa and Asia. Thus it was fought over throughout history, by ancient Canaanites, Egyptians, Israelites—and later by Napoleon, Allenby and the Israelis in 1948. Messianic thought of the

262. The Incense Altar (thirteenth century BC) Hazor. Height 0.40 m. basalt
Burn-marks on top of this pillar-like altar point to its use in the sacrifice of incense. The emblem on its front is similar to one appearing on the breast of a fragmentary basalt figure found in the same temple, and originally shown as standing on a bull: a storm-god, whose temple this must have been.

263. The Lioness Orthostat (sixteenth to fifteenth century BC) Hazor. Height 0.60 m. basalt
The head of one of the two orthostats—basalt slabs, left unworked at the back, being intended as part of the entrance-jambs of a temple—represents a lioness. This and other orthostats were found at Hazor in re-use in a temple of the thirteenth century BC, but were proved to have belonged to a much earlier temple. Today this impressive fragment stands in front of the Hazor Museum at Ayelet Ha-Shahar, while its male counterpart is in the Israel Museum, Jerusalem. This, as well as the two cult objects described above, clearly show a Syro-Hittite influence (see also pls. 24–5).

263

first century AD located Armageddon here, the place of the battle at the End of Days, before mankind's redemption (Rev. 16:16). The small site museum, at the foot of the mount, exhibits some of the finds from its twenty strata, representing three thousand years of history. While the major finds from its excavations are shown at the Rockefeller Museum, Jerusalem, the site museum has to concentrate on a display of large models and drawings which take into account the results of recent excavations at the site. These include a Canaanite 'high place', temples, a casement-wall and a gate of King Solomon's time, to which Megiddo's large water-system, connecting an outer source via an underground channel into the walled city, may be ascribed. It is, however, also possible that this system was built by King Omri and his son Ahab. The latter re-fortified the city in the second quarter of the ninth century BC and built large stables there for his chariot-horses. (It should be remembered that at the battle of Karkar in 853 BC against Shalmaneser III of Assyria, the army of the Syro-Israelite allies included some 2,000 of Ahab's chariots.)

Caesarea, on the shores of the Mediterranean, was built as a Roman city by King Herod in place of the Hellenistic townlet of Straton's Tower; it became the capital of the Roman governors from AD 6, and remained a provincial capital for some six hundred years. Throughout this period it had an important Jewish community and from the end of the second century AD was the see of a bishop. Priding itself on its superb library, it counted amongst its famous Christians one of the Fathers of the Church, Origenes (whose teachings were condemned by the Church in 553), and Eusebius, famous early in the fourth century not only for his theological and historical writings, but for his Onomasticon of Biblical place-names which still serves scholars today. The conquests of the Crusaders started the city's

264

264. Eagle and Lions Sarcophagus (third century BC) Beth Shearim. Length 2.60 m. stone
This heavy local imitation of a sarcophagus, common at the time in marble or stone throughout the Roman Empire, appears to have been a sort of status symbol and is interesting for its naïve but forceful execution. The sarcophagus comes from a chamber of the largest catacomb of this Jewish necropolis. Beth Shearim was at that time at the height of its fame, the seat of the Sanhedrin, the Jewish High Court, and its venerable President, Rabbi Judah, who died *c*. AD 220. Jews from many parts of the Diaspora transferred their relatives' last remains to this venerated spot for final interment. The town was destroyed by the Romans in 351 AD.

While the sarcophagi of the very pious omitted all representative art, the decorated ones shown here do not seem to have shocked the more tolerant spirit of the less orthodox. (see also pl. 54.)

decline, even though it had been fortified by Louis IX of France in the mid-thirteenth century.

Some results of the excavations may be seen both inside the fortress and outside its walls, including a beautiful Roman theatre, founded by King Herod and in use again today. Near the city's Crusader walls and flanking a Byzantine street, stand huge Roman imperial statues re-used by later rulers. At the site museum, located in the adjacent Kibbutz **Sdot Yam**, are exhibited very fine Roman statues, coins and lamps, as well as some interesting items from Crusader times.

Masada, above the Dead Sea, is probably one of the most spectacular sites in the country, though its history spans only three periods—that of its founder, King Herod, that of its Zealot defenders, and that of the late contemplators of its former fate, a group of Byzantine monks. It lay hidden for some 1300 years, to awaken to a very thorough exploration and excavation. The results may now be visited easily, the site museum at the foot of the rock serving admirably as an introduction.

Mamshit (Kurnub) is one of the Nabatean caravan-cities (easily reached today from Dimona), occupied by the Roman army and still extensively used in Byzantine times, as witnessed by some large churches excavated inside its well preserved walls. The small site museum contains finds from these periods. The main exhibit is, of course, the site itself: one walks down a deserted street, into a lonely courtyard and an empty room. Beyond lies a roofless church with its shattered altar, forever swept by the desert wind.

265. Fighting Wolves (beginning of third century BC) Beth Shearim. Length 0.60 m. stone

The detail shown here comes from the entrance arch of a mausoleum which stood in front of a spacious Jewish catacomb. Amongst other finds were the fragments of a marble sarcophagus (now at the Rockefeller Museum, Jerusalem), representing on its sides the myths of Achilles on Scyros, Leda and the Swan, and a hunt—probably Meleager hunting the Calydonian Boar. These mythological expressions of invincible fate and pre-ordained death seem natural enough in the contemporary pagan world, but strike us as strange in the framework of a third-century rabbinical centre in Israel.

This detail too, showing fighting wolves, seems very different in its imagery and style to anything else discovered locally. A Scythian or Sarmatian influence has been suggested, perhaps no more than an enlargement of some small decorative item. Such items originated in the second to third centuries in South Russia and the steppes beyond; some of them did, in fact, reach the shores of Syria-Palaestina in the first half of the third century AD, perhaps by way of the caravan-cities of Dura-Europos and Palmyra. The appearance of such foreign and indeed pagan images in a rabbinical Jewish setting can be explained by a certain cultural tolerance, discernible between the first century BC and the sixth AD, stemming from the fact that the pagan gods and their myths were no longer taken very seriously, having become mainly sources of literary or artistic imagery.

265 ·

266

MEGIDDO

266. Model of Megiddo
This large model summarizes the latest discoveries made at this important site during recent excavations. It shows the city during the second quarter of the ninth century BC under King Ahab. Part of his large chariot-units must have kept their horses in the extensive stables seen in the centre, while the mighty gate in the foreground, originally built by Solomon, is seen here as it was re-fortified by Ahab. The Canaanite high-place and temples of the nineteenth century BC (see following pl.) are in the deep cut to the right.

267

267. Megiddo Temples and High Place (twentieth to nineteenth centuries BC)

The deep excavation of the site of Megiddo revealed three temples, each consisting of a large chamber with an altar on the south side; the easternmost temple, built of mud-brick shows two pillar-bases at the corners of the altar. It is the earliest of these temples, facing East; the light of the sun rising over Mount Tabor and the Jordan Valley throws its first rays directly upon the altar—an early instance of sun-worship. The round high place (of some ten metres diameter), built of stone, with steps leading up to the platform, has its beginnings in 2700 BC. It continued in service when the temples were in use. It seems thus that the ancient concept of local gods, often worshipped in the form of some unhewn standing-stone (Masseba) placed on high, often near a tree and always under the open sky, was not easily relinquished. Even when different concepts of a god were introduced, the stone seems to have been kept in a mysterious dark chamber, appearing only rarely in procession when it would be shown to believers. In folk-belief the deity dwelt 'on every high hill and under every green tree' (1 K. 14:23; 2 K. 17:10; Jer. 2:20, etc.) and continued to do so to modern times, changing its form into some local saint, Christian or Moslem, whose tomb became a place of pilgrimage and veneration.

MASADA

268. Masada (first century BC–AD 73)
This site, above the West shore of the Dead Sea, though correctly identified in 1838, was only excavated to any great extent between 1963 and 1965. The fortress was built by King Herod about 30 BC and used by the Jews in AD 73 for their last stand against the Romans. In the sixth century it served for a while a group of Byzantine monks, who constructed a monastery in its ruins. The picture shows the north end of this rock-fortress, with the large storeroom on top; the roofed building is a magnificent bath. To the left is the northern palace, descending in three large terraces, with a fine view over the Dead Sea towards En Gedi. The openings in the rock-face lead into an elaborate system of water cisterns.

269

269. Masada Museum (1968)
Carefully built in shape and materials
attuned to the character of Masada,
this museum at the rock's eastern foot
exhibits explanatory material, models
and a sampling of the finds from the
site. In the foreground are some of
the many heavy stone missiles, which the
besieging Romans hurled against the
handful of defenders in AD 73.

CAESAREA SITE AND SDOT YAM MUSEUM

270. Imperial Statue (second century AD) Caesarea. Present height 2.45 m. Egyptian porphyry

This statue of a Roman Emperor was found re-used in a public square of Caesarea, built by a Byzantine city mayor in the sixth century. It is obvious that it was taken at that time from an earlier public building, and set up to grace the square. It must have lost its head, as so many statues of antiquity in the East, when later generations believed that their heathen forbears had hidden gold inside them. Even smashing the head did not really disillusion the treasure-hunters since it was thought that ancient magic had at the last moment turned the gold into rubble; at any rate, the smashing of the head, thus robbing the statue of possible diabolic influences, was considered a wise and good deed. The statue sits majestically in its tunic and toga; our imagination must add the long sceptre in its right hand and the orb in its left, as well as the diademed head. It has been convincingly argued that it originally represented the Emperor Hadrian, who visited his troops fighting in the second and final war against the Jews. It seems likely that a 'Hadrianeum' was established in the city during that visit made around AD 133; such a building was still referred to in the sixth century, when this statue could have been transferred to its present place.

270

271

272

271. a-b. Seal of Hugh Garnier (*c.* 1154–1167) Caesarea. Diam. 0.02 m. lead

The obverse (a) shows a knight, riding to the left, armed with an elongated shield and a lowered pennoned lance; the inscription reads: SIGILLUM UGONIS GRENARII. The reverse (b) shows the walls of Caesarea, with a large gate in its central tower, the inscription reading: CIVITAS CAESAREE. Hugh Garnier was second lord of this city. In 1164 King Amalric of Jerusalem sent him to Egypt at the head of a delegation to the young Al-Adid, last of the Fatimid Caliphs, and his mighty Vizir, Shirkuh. In Amalric's Egyptian campaign of 1167 Hugh was captured by Shirkuh and his nephew Saladin.

272. Caesarea's Crusader Fortifications (mid-thirteenth century)

Recently excavated and partly restored, these were built when King Louis IX of France visited the Holy Land in 1251–52. They comprise a strong wall, fortified with a glacis, towers, a moat and a counterscarp. Contemporary sources recount that the king himself took part in the construction. The fortifications withstood the first onslaught of Baybar's army, but were demolished in 1265 after the capitulation of their defenders.

SPECIALIZED MUSEUMS

While most of the museums so far mentioned are by their very nature mixed museums containing exhibits from many fields, some of those already mentioned are dedicated to a specialized subject as, for example, the Museum of Japanese Art and the Dagon Museum, both in Haifa. One should, however, mention some of the other specialized museums, in order to give a frame of reference to the achievements reached by Israeli museology in these fields.

Besides the museums noted above, the **Museum of Natural History** in Jerusalem should be mentioned. Jerusalem is also one of the few places in the world to have a **Tax Museum** appropriately enough housed in the central Customs offices. A small **Printers' Museum**, founded by the Printers' Union in 1953, was transferred from Jerusalem to Safed in 1961—a suitable move, since it was in Safed that the first Hebrew printing shop was established in 1577. Some early prints, as well as ancient printing presses, are on display there. **The Museum of Musical Instruments** in Jerusalem has a small but interesting collection of both Oriental and European instruments within the National Academy of Music. In Jerusalem too a small **Theatre Museum** has just been established.

In addition to Haifa's Japanese Art museum, mentioned above, the **Wilfrid Israel House of Oriental Art** contains some interesting collections. Situated at Ha-Zore'a, it has a double surprise for its visitors in the beautiful setting of the well-tended gardens and in an expertly organized exhibition of Chinese, Indian and Cambodian art, as well as some unique local antiquities. It also has a fine library and special exhibitions, frequently changed.

The Museum of Mediterranean Archaeology is located between Kibbutz Nir David and the Sakhne Nature Park, where running water and pleasant lawns surround a swimming pool. The museum's exhibitions include good artifacts of ancient Greek, Hellenistic, Roman and Italo-Etruscan art, as well as some rare examples of the art of Persia which range from antiquity to the Islamic period. In addition to this, antiquities discovered on the spot are shown, including a weaver's workshop of the eighth century BC. In both these cases it is interesting to note that, even in museums dedicated to very specialized fields, locally discovered antiquities find their place in the exhibition; the local and foreign complement one

WILFRID ISRAEL HOUSE OF ORIENTAL ART

273. Bodhisattva (twelfth century AD) Cambodia. Height 0.28 m. sandstone This beautiful Khmer head carries as head-dress a small Buddha. The eyes are closed as to an inner vision, the lips carry the light smile of the mystic. The sculpture expresses in simple lines the contemplative character of Buddhism.

221

274. Western Trader (seventh to eighth century AD) China. Height 0.22 m. terracotta

The many T'ang statuettes found in tombs of that period were intended to supply the dead with all their needs in the netherworld, a concept very similar to those held in earlier periods in Egypt (see pl. 205). These figurines include representations of traders, who came from Central and Western Asia and from India to offer their goods, and are here supplying the dead with coveted luxuries. Such trade seems to have started in the early first century AD, but became fairly extensive under the T'ang dynasty. The figurine shows a man carrying a pack on his shoulders, a jug in his left hand. Dressed in a belted coat and Western-style hat, he is bearded and his features suggest he is a Jewish trader. This assumption is strengthened by the fact that during the eighth and ninth centuries AD Jewish merchants, known as Radanites, did indeed carry out large-scale trade between the Frankish Kingdom of Western Europe, Africa and the Far East, either via the Red Sea and Arabia or Constantinople. They brought weapons and furs to the East, and precious metals, gems, spices and costly fabrics to the West.

274

another and connections can be seen which, but for this confrontation, would have been missed. The rural population has taken to these museums and they are now cultural centres for their district.

The L. A. Mayer Institute of Islamic Art in Jerusalem opened a museum in 1974, containing important items from Spain and North Africa to India. A valuable collection of rare watches forms a unique addition.

275

276

275. Maitreya With Attendants (sixth century AD) China. Height 0.48 m. stone

Maitreya (lit. 'the Benevolent') is a Bodhisattva conceived as the future Buddha; it is thus really a messianic concept, common to ancient Iran and India. The stele shown here belongs to a period when Buddhism had been absorbed by China. The figure is sitting in front of a leaf-shaped mandorla, a copy in stone of similar steles executed at that time in bronze. It seems likely that such steles were painted; their presentation to a temple—indeed their manufacture —was considered a meritorious deed.

276. Guardian of the World (seventh to eighth century AD) China. Height 0.99 m. terracotta, largely glazed; remains of colour on unglazed parts

Such statues stood inside the entrance of the tomb-caves of T'ang tombs and were intended to protect the deceased, his coffin and the many statuettes placed there as attendants. This guardian is shown standing in victory over a bull, symbolizing the evil spirits who tried to rape the soul of the deceased. The origin of the concept must be sought in Hinduism where Yama—the first to die and enter the netherworld—became

'King of Righteousness', judge of the deceased, eventually becoming the god who ruled over the souls of the dead in the underworld, between their death and rebirth. Buddhism regarded him as a guardian deity. As such he entered China, where Buddhism reached supremacy under the T'ang dynasty in the seventh to eighth centuries AD.

223

277

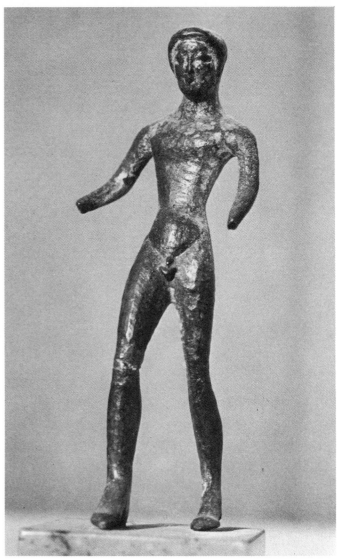

278

MUSEUM OF MEDITER-RANEAN ARCHAEOLOGY

277. Helmet (fifth century BC) Italy. Height 0.14 m. bronze

A fine Greek helmet from Lucania, expressing something of the fierce spirit of the Greek settlers, merchants, seamen and often pirates, who constantly fought Etruscans and Carthaginians for supremacy of rule and trade. The former pressed down upon the Greeks from North and Central Italy, while the latter waxed strong in North Africa, Sardinia, the Balearic Islands and Sicily. Greek trade, however, was prospering on the north-east coast of Italy and the south of Gaul. Waves of newcomers from Ionia pressed meanwhile into southern Italy and Etruria. The eventual rise of Rome, sweeping all these off the map, was still far below the horizon.

278. Walking Youth (beginning of fifth century BC) Italy. Height 0.08 m. bronze

This lively Graeco-Campanian figurine was manufactured by a local Greek artist at a time when Greek settlers were struggling with Etruscans pressing down the peninsula, and with Carthaginians at the height of their power in the Mediterranean. It is interesting to compare the high artistic level of these minor pieces with the mediocrity of most of the monumental sculpture of the Western Greeks, who were much inferior in this to their progressive Aegean contemporaries.

279. *Colour plate II.* **The Dancers' Jar** (4000–3200 BC) En el Jarba. Height 0.27 m. pottery (Wilfrid Israel House)

This hole-mouth jar is unique in Israel, and was accidentally discovered near Kibbutz Ha-Zore'a, in the Esdraelon Plain. On both sides the jar carries in relief a dancing figure, its animal head, presumably a mask, turned to the side; between the legs the male member is represented. Fertility-dances or hunting-dances with animal-masks, fundamentally totemistic, are common to many cultures and periods. The nearest in time and place to this find was discovered some years ago at Tepe Gawra in Iraq. It is possible that this jar, like so much of the culture of the period, points to links with the north. (For representations of dances and ceremonies at a slightly later period, but connected with the hunt and found near Ha-Zore'a, see pl. 211.)

280

280. Persian Royal Attendant (fifth century BC) Persepolis. Height 0.21 m. stone
Darius ruled from 521 to 485 BC as King of Kings of the Persian Empire, reaching from India to Sardis and from South Russia to the Sudan. At Persepolis he built his central residence, though its majestic royal council hall—the Apadana—was finished only under his successor Xerxes I (485–465 BC). It was at this time that the Jews were able to return from their exile to Jerusalem and re-dedicate their Temple. The Palace, the Harem, the Treasury and the Apadana were adorned with a large number of reliefs, many showing Persian and Median noblemen, guards and attendants, serving the king or introducing foreign delegations to the King's feasts. The photograph shows the head of one such Persian attendant, perhaps carrying gifts for the king, or attending to his commands at an audience.

225

281

THE L. A. MAYER MEMORIAL INSTITUTE OF ISLAMIC ART

281. Seljuk Unglazed Bowl (twelfth century AD) Iran. Height 0.11 m. pottery
This deep bowl has a moulded decoration showing human figures, some bearded, sitting cross-legged, or with one foot propped up. The upper frieze shows pairs of birds, while the lower has a *guilloche* and a scroll ornament. (The Metropolitan Museum of Art in New York has a large collection of such vessels, coming from Nishapur in Iran, which was at that time a centre for this type of pottery.) The Seljuk Turks originally came from the Kirkhiz steppes of Turkestan. They advanced in the tenth and eleventh centuries[1] through Bukhara, accepting Sunnite Islam, and then into Iran, reaching Isfahan *c.* AD 1037. Their further progress brought them to Baghdad, where the Caliph received the Seljuk ruler

Tughril as regent of the Empire, titled officially *al-sultan*, the first to bear this title. Further conquests added Armenia and large tracts of Asia Minor, Syria and Palestine to the lands of these sultans.

This bowl belongs to the period of the disintegration of the Seljuk Empire, though each branch held its own provinces in Iran and Iraq to the end of the twelfth century. The main contribution of the Seljuks to the Islamic culture was as patrons of the arts.

282. *Colour plate XLV.* **Ilkhan Casket** (second half of the thirteenth century AD) Iran. Height 0.12 m. brass, silver and gold inlay
The rectangular casket, its high lid hinged, shows two medallions with representations of falconers, sitting drinking near small tables; all is done in beautiful inlay-work, on a background richly decorated with tendrils and geometric roundels. The lower centre has two juxtaposed harpies. The first to bear the title of *Ilkhan* was Hulegu, Ghengis Khan's grandson, who moved out of Mongolia in 1256, crushed the Assassin strongholds, including their centre Alamut in North Iran and, a year later, put an end to Baghdad's Abbasid Caliphate. The rule of his successors continued to the beginning of the fourteenth century, their centre being at Maragha on the south-west corner of the Caspian Sea. They established there a rich library and an observatory, maintaining a group of Persian scholars and artists at their court.

283

HISTORY MUSEUMS

A peculiar fact in the long history of the Jewish people is the lack of any comprehensive history museum of its own in Israel. The obvious reasons for this situation were pointed out at the beginning of the book: dispersion, persecution and lack of secure abode for any length of time were not conducive to collection, preservation, and display. In as far as documents and artifacts of value survive, they are mostly in archives and museums abroad. For this reason these museums have had to concentrate their interest on recent history, the resettlement and establishment of modern Israel, a period of some one hundred years. They contain two events which to many seem messianic: the destruction of six million Jews; and the establishment of a free and independent Israel. As stated earlier (p.175), the city-museum of Petah Tiqva exhibits the earliest remains of this period, dating from 1878 when the city was founded by a group of Jews from Jerusalem, in order to 'till the soil and fulfil the commandments pertaining to it; for the furtherance of the honour of Israel and that it may never again be degraded amongst the nations'. Documents, photos and settlers' implements and utensils revive memories of this period. Early communal settlements of the country, the kibbutzim, are represented in various kibbutz museums, some of which were mentioned when describing the Hanitha and Beth Sturman museums at En Harod.

283. Herzl Museum—his study
This room formed part of the Vienna flat of Theodor Herzl, founder of Zionism, where he lived from the 1880s to his death in 1904. The Zionist organization later transferred it to Germany, later still to Jerusalem, where it was kept in the main offices of the Jewish Agency. In 1960 it was included in the museum, dedicated to Herzl and his work, which was set up on its present site on the western slope of Mount Herzl.

Kefar Giladi and nearby Tel Hai are others which were dedicated to the freedom movement's early days when, after the 1903 massacre of the Jews in Kishinev, Russia, a group of young Jewish immigrants from Russia banded together within the new labour movement to form an organization for self-defence named Ha-Shomer (the watchman), which eventually established its own settlements. Kibbutz Yif'at has lately established a fine museum, exhibiting local developments in agriculture from the beginning of this century to the present, and reconstructing the early days of life on a kibbutz. Here is demonstrated the first stage, when the members were still living in tents in the malaria-infested swamps of the Yezreel valley, and the second phase, when wooden huts began to be used, at least for the communal dining-hall. Again, one meets the now familiar phenomenon of Jewish history: the fact that the really important part of kibbutz life—the spirit of devotion, simplicity and brotherhood—cannot be shown because of its intangibility.

The Jews' physical struggle for survival in two world wars and in local clashes is exhibited in Israel's army museums: at Beth Golomb in Tel Aviv, where the story of the Haganah, the self-defence of the Jews between 1921 and 1948, the story of the Jewish Brigade of the second world war and of Israel's young army of 1948 are told, both

284. Herzl's Tomb
His remains were transferred to a hill to the west of Jerusalem in 1949. The site, overlooking the hills of Judah, has been known ever since as Mount Herzl.

285. Petah Tiqva Museum
Originally founded as a war memorial (*Yad Lebanim*: 'Memorial to the Sons'), the Municipal Museum here has grown into a fully-fledged museum, dividing its interest between art—temporary exhibitions being mainly shown—and the story of the city's founders, i.e., the founders of the Jewish settlements in Israel one hundred years ago. Part of the history section of the museum can be seen here, showing artifacts, documents and photographs of the city's early days when it was founded in 1878 by a group of Jews from Jerusalem.

at **Avihayil** in the Sharon plain where relics of the Jewish Brigade of the 1914–1918 war are exhibited, and in Haifa, where the immigrant ship, **Af-Al-Pi-Chen**, includes items connected with Israel's navy.

Aaronson House at Zikhron Ya'akov has its very special place amongst the museums of this country: it is dedicated to a family who were the founders of this vintners' village in 1882; one of the sons of the family—Aaron—was the scholar who discovered *Triticum dicoccoides*, a species of corn still growing wild in this country and considered by many scholars to be the ancient 'mother wheat'. In 1917 he and his sister Sara led a small group of local volunteers to assist the advancing British army, the latter sacrificing her life in this enterprise. The house is exhibited exactly as it stood between 1882 and 1917, a style in which Russian, French, Turkish, Arabic and Jewish traits are strangely mixed; a setting which has succeeded in some eerie way in freezing time.

The underground movements of the fight against British rule in this country maintain the **Jabotinski Museum** in Tel Aviv and in the former central prisons of Jerusalem and Acre, where underground fighters were incarcerated and some executed.

Both an historical and site museum, the **Herzl Museum** stands

286. Aaronson House
Parts of the mansion of the Aaronson family, founders in 1882 of this village of vineyards, Zihron Ya'akov, have been opened as a museum. It includes a fine herbarium, and also an exhibition concerning the lives of members of this family, and the 'Nili' group of activists who, in 1917, aided the British forces in their advance into Israel, at that time still held by the Turks. The house —this is a view from the drawing-room towards Aaron Aaronson's study—has been left as it was in 1917, when one of the daughters of the house—Sara— committed suicide rather than disclose to the Turks the secrets of their group, of which she was a central member.

287

287. Kibbutz Yif'at dining-hall
(nineteen-twenties)
The dining-hall of a kibbutz, a simple
wooden hut, was used by the community
for many functions besides eating. The
spinning-wheels for instance, seen in the
background, were kept whirring by
the women, providing the raw material
for clothing sewn in the room at the far
background, which was used also as
kitchen. The dining-hall was also used
for all the community's social occasions:
the general assembly, which decided on
all major matters concerning the Kibbutz and its members; and the festivi-
ties, when song and dance would be led
by music from the accordion, held here
by the Museum's curator. It is interesting to compare the stark simplicity of
these early kibbutz interiors with the
ornate drawing-rooms of the wealthy
farmers at the beginning of the century
(see previous plate).

on a slope of the hill now called Mount Herzl, in Jerusalem. It is dedicated to Theodor Herzl, the Viennese journalist and writer of light comedies, charming stories and essays, who in 1895, after reporting to his paper the unjust condemnation and degradation of a young Jewish captain in the French army, Alfred Dreyfus, with mobs roaming the streets of Paris outside shouting 'Death to the Jews!', sat down to write a pamphlet, *The Jewish State*, and forged the instrument for its establishment: the Zionist Movement. He convened this movement's first congress in Basle in 1897: in his diary, he noted simply: 'At Basle I founded the Jewish State . . . perhaps in some five years, certainly in fifty years everyone will acknowledge it.' His study has been re-assembled in this museum; the story of his life and the evidence of his political struggles are well told in the exhibition. Fifty-two years after that diary entry, his remains were brought from Vienna and buried on the wind-swept hill nearby, overlooking the Mountains of Judah. This is the spot from which fire-signals annually proclaim the eve of Israel's Independence Day.

To the west of the Mount stands a very different museum and memorial: **Yad Vashem**, memorial to the victims of the Holocaust, founded by an Act of the Knesset in 1953; its museum re-opened in 1973. This is the largest of the three museums in the country dedicated to the theme of the destruction and extermination of Europe's Jews by Nazi Germany, the two others being **Lohamei Hageta'ot**

288. Exterior of Beth Lohamei Hageta'ot (1959)
This 'House of the Ghetto-Fighters' was established by remnants of the Jewish partisans in their kibbutz of the same name, in memory of one of their leaders, Ishak Katzenelson, poet and partisan, who fell in the fight; and in memory of all those whom they had seen in agony and death. It is literally filled to the roof-beams with the detailed documentation of that horror.

289

289. Exterior of Yad Vashem, Jerusalem

The central museum is housed in the lower foreground, a mural relief by Naftali Bezem (born 1924) in front of it. This, as well as the memorial pylon in the background, repeats the motif of the chimney-stack of the crematories:

'O you chimneys
O you fingers
And Israel's body in smoke through
    the air'

as Nelly Sachs says in her poem, citing Job 19:26: 'And when after my skin this is destroyed, then without my flesh shall I see God.'

In the left background is the memorial hall, its floor covered with names—Sobibor, Belzec, Treblinka, Auschwitz.

in the north and **Yad Mordekhai** in the south. While their theme is the same, each has its own approach to this subject still uppermost in the minds of some of the Jews of our generation. The Lohamei Hageta'ot ('Ghetto-Fighters') were such partisans who managed to survive and reach the shores of Israel. The main aim in establishing their kibbutz was the foundation of a museum in fulfilment of the vow that survivors would keep a record for posterity of what they had seen. This they have done in a dedicated and unswerving manner, in huge halls filled with stark horror. **Yad Vashem** (lit. 'Monument and Memorial'), which keeps the official records of that terrible period, has succeeded in concentrating a full picture of former Jewish life, mainly in Eastern Europe, its destruction, and the full tragedy of human brutality towards six million innocent and helpless Jews, of whom one and a half million were children. It must be considered one of the most difficult visits to any museum in the world; even Hiroshima's horrifying museum shows only a moment of horror perpetrated by man without facing his victim. Here, however, we have man inflicting his deeds meticulously, deliberately and consciously; facing his victim at all the stages of his calvary, six million times, while the world stood apart, leaving the victim to a terrible loneliness in his agony and death.

Yad Mordekhai starts its exhibition with reminders of the Jewish townlet in Eastern Europe and describes the stages on the way to the

233

gas-ovens. The exhibition continues the story with the Jews' struggle to reach the shores of their land, establish their settlements, and fight for survival. It depicts the heroic fight of this small kibbutz against a large invading Egyptian army in 1948, when finally the few surviving defenders had to retreat. A glance through the well-kept lawns, however, where happy toddlers play with parents who have returned from work in the fields, adds brighter hues to this sombre picture. It may well be that building a museum dealing with death in utter despair, within a setting of life and confidence, expresses that absolute Jewish rejection of the defiling and degrading uncleanness of death, setting against it its messianic belief in life everlasting.

290. Inside the Museum

This photo was taken on one of Jerusalem's beautiful, sunny days. A very old lady was walking behind us, softly moaning: she had suffered through the holocaust—and had survived. In front of us walked a young tourist, who had come in largely ignorant of all that happened, like most of us. Tears stood in her wide-open eyes, wanting to disbelieve the evidence of this chapter of man's recent history.

291. The Headstones

This final hall of the museum uses the ancient form of Jewish headstones to display the names of countries, together with the numbers of their exterminated Jews. A glass-case, set into the stone that commemorates the deaths of one and a half million children, holds a baby's shoe, out of a pile of many thousands found in one of the extermination-camps.

291

292

292. Interior of the Yad Mordekhai Memorial

Named in memory of Mordekhai Anielevic, leader of the Warsaw Ghetto's fight against the Nazis in 1943, this kibbutz built a museum in 1965, recounting the story of the Eastern-European Jewish communities, their life, the extermination of their great majority, the fight of the partisans and the return of the survivors to their ancient homeland—Israel. The exhibition ends with the section shown here: the struggle of the new Kibbutz, founded in 1943, against the might of the Egyptian army who besieged it in 1948 and occupied it for some weeks until driven back by Israel's army. Time has healed the wounds: a view out of the Museum's windows shows the children and grandchildren of those sufferers and fighters, seen in the Museum's exhibition, playing on the lawn.

293. New Horizons (1973); Youth Wing, Israel Museum, Jerusalem
'*And the streets of the city shall be full of boys and girls playing in the streets thereof*' (Zech. 8:5). Children painting a large mural on one of the walls of the Israel Museum. Perhaps some of these children will grow up to create masterpieces which will grace the walls of the museums of the future.

293

CHRONOLOGICAL TABLE

Prehistoric Periods

Cultural stage:

	BC
Palaeolithic	500,000–15,000
Mesolithic	15,000– 8000
Neolithic	8000– 4000
Chalcolithic	4000– 3150

Archaeological and Historic Periods

	BC
Early Canaanite	3150–2200
Middle Canaanite	2200–1550
Late Canaanite	1550–1200
Israelite	1200– 586
Babylonian/Persian	586– 332
Hellenistic	332– 152
Hellenistic (Hasmonean)	152– 37
Roman (Herodian)	37–AD 70

	AD
Roman	70– 324
Byzantine	324– 640
Early Arab	640–1099
Crusader	1099–1291
Mamluk	1291–1516
Turkish	1516–1917
British Mandatory	1917–1948